CONVERSATIONS ON QUENTIN TARANTINO

by Andrew J. Rausch

Chris Watson, Contributing Editor

Conversations on Quentin Tarantino
©2016 Andrew J. Rausch

All rights reserved.

No part of this book may be reproduced in any form or by any means, electronic, mechanical, digital, photocopying, or recording, except for inclusion of a review, without permission in writing from the publisher.

Published in the USA by:

BearManor Media
P.O. Box 71426
Albany, Georgia 31708
www.BearManorMedia.com

ISBN-10: 1-59393-964-7 (alk. paper)
ISBN-13: 978-1-59393-964-9 (alk. paper)

Front cover photo courtesy of Photofest 2016
Back cover photo courtesy of Dreamstime 2016

Design and Layout: Valerie Thompson

Other BearManor Media books by Andrew J. Rausch

The Stephen King Movie Quiz Book (with R.D. Riley)
The Wit & Wisdom of Stephen King
Dirty Talk: Conversations with Porn Stars (with Chris Watson)
Gods of Grindhouse: Interviews with Exploitation Filmmakers
The Godfather of Gore Speaks (with Herschell Gordon Lewis)
The Cinematic Misadventures of Ed Wood
(with Charles E. Pratt, Jr.)
Trash Cinema: A Celebration of Overlooked Masterpieces
(with R.D. Riley)

"I'm a big fan of violence in cinema. I believe that Thomas Edison invented the camera to film people beating the shit out of each other."
—*Quentin Tarantino*

TABLE OF CONTENTS

Complete Filmography . . . 1

Foreword #1: "The Giddy Glee of Quentin T" . . . 5
by Stephen J. Spignesi

Foreword #2: "A Flashback is a Flashback" . . . 9
by C. Courtney Joyner

Introduction: "Do Go *Hateful* Into This Good Night" . . . 15
by Jason Pankoke

Author's Note by Andrew J. Rausch . . . 19

1. Jami Bernard . . . 21
2. Larry Bishop . . . 25
3. Paul Calderon . . . 33
4. Omar Doom . . . 39
5. R.M. Guera . . . 45
6. Sid Haig . . . 51
7. Craig Hamann . . . 57
8. Monte Hellman . . . 63
9. Dennis Humbert . . . 67
10. Angela Jones . . . 73

11. **Linda Kaye** ... 77
12. **Robert Kurtzman** ... 87
13. **Steve Martinez** ... 91
14. **Don Murphy** ... 97
15. **P.J. Pesce** ... 103
16. **Tom Savini** ... 111
17. **Tony Scott** ... 119
18. **Scott Spiegel** ... 125
19. **Guillermo del Toro** ... 133
20. **Bill Unger** ... 139
21. **Rand Vossler** ... 151
22. **Matt Wagner** ... 165
23. **Duane Whitaker** ... 173
24. **Mike White** ... 179

Index ... 187

About the Contributors ... 195

COMPLETE FILMOGRAPHY

Quentin Jerome Tarantino
Born: March 27, 1963

DIRECTOR

1. *Reservoir Dogs* (1992)
2. *Pulp Fiction* (1994)
3. *Four Rooms*: "The Man from Hollywood" (1995)
4. *E.R.* Episode: "Motherhood" (1995) [TV]
5. *Jackie Brown* (1997)
6. *Kill Bill: Volume 1* (2003)
7. *Kill Bill: Volume 2* (2004)
8. *Jimmy Kimmel Live!* episode: #3.75 (2004) [TV]
9. *Sin City* (2005) [as Special Guest Director]
10. *CSI: Crime Scene Investigation*: episodes: "Grave Danger: 1 & 2" (2005) [TV]
11. *Grindhouse/Death Proof* (2007)
12. *Inglourious Basterds* (2009)
13. *Django Unchained* (2012)
14. *The Hateful Eight* (2015)

PRODUCER

1. *Past Midnight* (1992) AP
2. *Killing Zoe* (1994) EP
3. *Four Rooms* (1995) EP
4. *From Dusk Till Dawn* (1996) EP
5. *Curdled* (1996) EP
6. *God Said, Ha!* (1997) EP
7. *From Dusk Till Dawn 2: Texas Blood Money* (1999) EP
8. *From Dusk Till Dawn 3: The Hangman's Daughter* (1999) EP
9. *Iron Monkey* (2001) P (re-release only)

10. *My Name is Modesty* (2004) EP
11. *Hostel* (2005) EP
12. *Daltry Calhoun* (2005) EP
13. *Freedom's Fury* (2006) EP
14. *Grindhouse/Deathproof/Planet Terror* (2007) P
15. *Hostel: Part II* (2007) EP
16. *Hell Ride* (2008) EP

SCREENWRITER

1. *Dance Me to the End of Love* (1992)
2. *Reservoir Dogs* (1992)
3. *Past Midnight* (1992) uncredited rewrites
4. *True Romance* (1993)
5. *Pulp Fiction* (1994)
6. *Natural Born Killers* (1994) story
7. *It's Pat* (1994) uncredited rewrites
8. *Four Rooms*: "The Man from Hollywood" (1995)
9. *Crimson Tide* (1995) uncredited rewrites
10. *From Dusk Till Dawn* (1996)
11. *Jackie Brown* (1997)
12. *Kill Bill: Vol. 1* (2003)
13. *Kill Bill: Vol. 2* (2004)
14. *CSI: Crime Scene Investigation*: episodes: "Grave Danger: 1 & 2" (2005) [TV]
15. *Grindhouse/Deathproof* (2007)
16. *Inglourious Basterds* (2009)
17. *Django Unchained* (2012)
18. *The Hateful Eight* (2015)

ACTOR FILMOGRAPHY

1. *Warzone* (1981) low-budget Super-8 film
2. *The Golden Girls*: episode "Sophia's Wedding" (1988) [TV]
3. *Dance Me to the End of Love* (1992)
4. *Reservoir Dogs* (1992)
5. *Eddie Presley* (1992)
6. *Somebody to Love* (1994)
7. *Sleep with Me* (1994)
8. *Pulp Fiction* (1994)

9. *All-American Girl*: episode "Pulp Sitcom" (1994) [TV]
10. *The Coriolis Effect* (1994) [voice only]
11. *Four Rooms* (1995)
12. *Destiny Turns on the Radio* (1995)
13. *Desperado* (1995)
14. *Girl 6* (1996)
15. *From Dusk Till Dawn* (1996)
16. *Jackie Brown* (1997) [uncredited answering machine voice]
17. *Full Tilt Boogie* (1997)
18. *Little Nicky* (2000)
19. *Alias* (2002-2004) [various episodes]
20. *Grindhouse/Deathproof/Planet Terror* (2007)
21. *Sukiyaki Western Django* (2007)
22. *Inglourious Basterds* (2009) [uncredited]
23. *Django Unchained* (2012)
24. *The Hateful Eight* (2015) [narrator]

EARLY AND UNCOMPLETED PROJECTS

1. *Captain Peachfuzz and the Anchovy Bandit* (1984) unfinished screenplay
2. *Lovebirds in Bondage* (1985) uncompleted film, co-written and directed with Scott McGill
3. *My Best Friend's Birthday* (1986) uncompleted film, co-written and directed with Craig Hamann
4. *Criminal Mind* (1986) treatment, co-written with Craig Hamann
5. Untitled western film (1988) concept, notes
6. *Undercover Elvis* (1988) concept, notes
7. *The Neon Jungle* (1988) treatment

FOREWORD #1: THE GIDDY GLEE OF QUENTIN T

by Stephen J. Spignesi

My favorite Quentin Tarantino film is *Pulp Fiction*. No, wait. Both volumes of *Kill Bill*. No, wait. *Jackie Brown*. No, wait. *Reservoir Dogs*. No…

Fuck.

"You must have big rats if you need Hattori Hanzo's steel."

How many of you just said "Huge"?

"Zed's dead, baby. Zed's dead."

And Fabienne got her pancakes. Buttermilk instead of blueberry, though.

"Look at you and your free ass."

Yes, Beaumont's ass was free, but it wasn't alive and free for very long.

"Wiggle your big toe."

Who else but QT would give us as much time as we needed to lovingly gaze at Uma Thurman's feet?

"Catch up."

One episode? He couldn't shoot one lousy episode of Fox Force Five*? Hell, he did an entire animated sequence about O-Ren for* Kill Bill*. Twenty or so minutes of TV during the shooting of a feature film would probably have been cheaper.*

"I mean all the time, morning, day, night, afternoon, dick, dick, dick, dick, dick, dick, dick, dick, dick, dick, dick."

"How many dicks is that?"

"A lot."

"Like a Virgin" is a metaphor for big dicks? *I always thought it was about a girl finding the love of her life. But big dicks works, too, I suppose.*

The Delfonics.
'Nuff said.
"Say 'what' again!"
Big Brain Brett should not have said "what" again.
"You mean you want to name your horse Tony?"
Django certainly did want to name his horse Tony, and Dr. Schulz believed the horse wore the name well.

There is, undeniably, something about a Quentin Tarantino film that induces obsession. *Serious* obsession.

There is also something about a Quentin Tarantino film that transcends mere appeal, enjoyment, and interest. A new Tarantino film—in the only comparisons I can make that come close to the anticipation and excitement generated—hits us like a new Beatles album, a new Stephen King novel, or new episodes of *Breaking Bad* or *The Sopranos*.

A Tarantino film falls into what I've come to call the "sight unseen" category. If I haven't had a chance to see a Tarantino film in the theater, I will buy the DVD the moment it becomes available. It's the same with me for a Stephen King book; it was the same for me with a Beatles album.

This bespeaks an extraordinary relationship between artist and fan, wouldn't you say?

And why is this? Because Quentin Tarantino has done what only the best artists ever achieve: he has morphed into an adjective.

Dickens-esque.
Warhol-esque.
Stephen King-ish.
Tarantino-esque.

You know what each of these mean, don't you? Think about the razor-sharp, crystal clear identification of an artist's style on the part of readers, viewers, or listeners required for his or her work to be used as an adjective to describe an entire genre or style of art.

My dear friend Sean Stevens, New Haven artist and cinephile, had this to say during one of our many conversations about writing, and movies and photography, and movies, and books, and movies and, of course, QT:

Foreword #1: The Giddy Glee of Quentin T

Tarantino's primary appeal is a funhouse aesthetic rooted in the spectacles of the early cinema days of nickelodeons grafted on to a literary point of entry in regard to storytelling with multiple characters and storylines. Not surprisingly, a trademark of his early films were a slacker aesthetic that juxtaposed lowbrow humor with ultraviolence.

Sean is right, but there's more. And in a word, it's that Tarantino's work makes us giddy.

Giddy with excitement, with joy, with enthusiasm. Quentin Tarantino makes movies that are fun. Big fun. Huge fun. Fun the size of the Bride's rats, so to speak.

Some other directors have done this, of course, with Martin Scorsese immediately coming to mind. (The "Get your fuckin' shine box" scene? Damn, that was fun.)

QT excels in the creation of fully-realized universes, as well as characters who jump off the screen and who spout dialogue so *awesome*, some of it becomes instantly a part of our long-term memory.

- "I'm American, honey. Our names don't mean shit."

- "We got a German here who wants to die for his country. Oblige him!"

- "And I will strike down upon thee with great vengeance and furious anger those who would attempt to poison and destroy my brothers."

- "Now that there is the Tec-9, a crappy spray gun from South Miami. This gun is advertised as the most popular gun in American crime. Do you believe that shit?"

This collection of interviews about the Master is a masterful look at one of the most brilliant, groundbreaking, and iconic writers and directors of our time.

Reading this informed, informative, and illuminating chats is almost as good as watching a QT film.

Almost.

But then again, not much really comes close to watching a QT film, right?

"I got no problem with that."

FOREWORD #2: A FLASHBACK IS A FLASHBACK
by C. Courtney Joyner

"Yeah, he's an okay kid."

With that statement, the inferno between Quentin Tarantino and Lawrence Tierney was finally extinguished, and I breathed a sigh of relief. It was Larry's birthday, and I thought the best present I could get him was a peace-offering call from Quentin, after their bloody head butting during, and after, the filming of *Reservoir Dogs*.

I asked Quentin to call Larry, and he did. They talked for almost twenty minutes.

This was a few years after that infamous jewel robbery flick, and Quentin's success was rocketing, and our history was fading. But he came through.

A few years led up to that call, starting, of course, with my first meeting Quentin, which seemed to be at Scott Spiegel's rented house in Hollywood. Quentin was a buddy of Scott's, and we'd met, lounged around Scott's living room a few times, and talked movies. Talked at high-speed, of course. The enthusiasms never stopped: he was a fan of *Prison*, and we tossed opinions running from Hong Kong action to Phil Karlson's best—quite a list there, and we could never agree—to Ingrid Pitt's coolest moments in *Where Eagles Dare*. And then, one of us would mention another flick, and away we went again.

Lots of arguing, and lots of agreements. Always pulling our own obscure references to secure our points and, in our movie-geek way, a friendship.

Quentin was writing, of course, and trying to put together some indie money for a couple of projects, but hadn't had anything made. I had just come off a divorce sabbatical in North Carolina, and was looking for some representation to help me get back some professional screenwriting cred, and he brought me to Cathryn Jaymes.

No telling of a Quentin tale is complete without Cathryn. She was his true champion, right from the start, way before anyone ever looked twice at the ex-video store clerk. She knew. And believed. And he loved her for it. They were as close as brother and sister, and when he brought me to her, and she signed me, it was a real endorsement, even though *Reservoir Dogs* was still in everyone's future.

Blonde, beautiful, funny, sensitive, remarkably loyal, and blade-sharp-smart, Cathryn was the perfect fit for Quentin. And, his friends. Roger Avary and the extraordinary Craig Hamann were all collaborating with Quentin in one form or another, while folks like Don Murphy, Jane Hamsher, Sheldon Lettich, Ron Zwang, Scott Spiegel, and Duane Whitaker also worked their magic on various projects, with and without Quentin, but with Cathryn touching every single project.

I mention this not to name-drop so much as to show that Cathryn's gang was a real community of filmmakers who helped each other, were part of each other's projects, as well as being good friends. Scripts were exchanged, notes given, lots of drinks downed, and more than a few late-night breakfasts gobbled while talking about movies, writing, and movies. Everyone was creating, and lots of us were shooting. The energy never stopped. A few keystrokes at Google, and its amazing to see how everyone's name intersects. Inside this circle was the perfect place for Quentin to thrive, and that's exactly what he did.

I was one of the first people to read an early draft of *Reservoir Dogs*, and on its second page, something jumped out: Lawrence Tierney's name. Not that Quentin was already thinking of casting Larry, but he'd loved the beyond-tough noirs that Larry had made at RKO in the 1940s, had been highly influenced by them, and knew Larry's reputation as a true American bad-ass. So, as an introduction to his script, he put his name on a roster of people, including Raoul Walsh and Don Siegel, whose work had inspired him to write *Dogs*.

But Quentin thought Larry was dead.

He got very excited, imagining Larry had been gunned down in some rainy back alley, or got shivved in a jail cell, but he never dreamed he lived in an apartment behind the Hollywood Library, and that we were good friends. So good, in fact, that with all our time together, many assumed I was his grandson. Friends Ron Zwang and Jeff Burr also confirmed that Larry was, indeed, very much above ground, and Quentin wanted, needed, to meet him.

Volumes could be written about Lawrence Tierney, and a few have tried to capture who he was, but all seem to miss it. They didn't know Larry, certainly not well, and the bullshit surrounding him, and his legend, looms large and wades deep. Movie star, convict, son of a police officer, brother of an actor, brawler, drunken menace, great friend, father, amazingly sensitive, literate, and truly wise. These puny words don't begin to touch on who Larry was. He crammed the lives of fifty into his own, living on the raw edge, but appreciating, and loving, the finer things in life. No stranger to either celebrity, fame, or infamy, he'd truly gone from the gutter to the penthouse and back again. He had had it all, and that gave him amazing perspective.

Larry was also one of the most loyal and generous people I ever knew, despised Hollywood bullshit, and possessed a whip-fast intelligence that could be as dangerous as his well-hammered fists. He was the real deal, and that's what Quentin wanted.

So, at my Christmas Party two months later, they were brought together. Lawrence Tierney was big, bald, and alive, and Quentin couldn't stop peppering him with questions. Larry always appreciated people who appreciated his work. Above all else, he was an actor who took pride in his profession, so this "excited kid" was okay with him.

When *Dogs* started shooting, I sent Quentin a telegram—the first he'd ever received, he told me—and I drove to the set, where they were shooting the opening scene in the diner that involved the entire cast, and trouble was already in the air. Larry was tense, and Quentin wasn't helping. Larry had a thing about being touched, particularly from behind, if it was someone he didn't know well, or trust. This was very old school, old street, and the fists would come up automatically. He didn't swing, but it was a defensive reflex. Eddie Bunker, also in the cast, and who'd done his time in a cage, understood it. Quentin didn't. Not really. He'd direct Larry by taking him by the shoulders, and positioning him for the camera, instead of simply telling him. The shots were specific, and Larry could be a little loose with his marks, but he'd get there, but Quentin needed his shots and positions for his actors. The fuses were burning. Even though I was supposed to stay for lunch, I left, and by the time I got home, maybe half an hour later, the phone was ringing, and Larry told me he'd been fired.

From what I could tell, from Larry's side, Quentin adjusted him again, they got into an argument, and a fist almost flew. Quentin told Larry to walk, amid approval from crew and disagreement from the cast. Larry was bringing something to Quentin's heist movie, and they all knew it, whatever the pain. Larry was steaming, and wanted to meet that night for some drinks. I knew that could end up badly, but before we could make other plans, Quentin and Laurence Bender called in, and Larry was back on the movie. The budget was so low, they really couldn't afford to re-cast, but I think Quentin also knew that what he was getting from Larry had genuine, bleeding truth to it, and he didn't want to let that go.

Larry stayed on *Dogs*, but not without incident. A nuclear incident. We didn't get together for drinks, but Larry went on a tear through Hollywood that led to another arrest, and this time, for really serious charges. Gunfire had been involved, and Larry had pushed the situation to the wall, just like one of Quentin's characters would have. However, the big issue was for myself, Larry's agent, and Cathryn Jaymes to get Larry bailed out of jail and back on the set Monday morning without Quentin or Laurence finding out about it. This was all happening on a Sunday afternoon, and we did it. Amazingly.

Working with Larry was kind of a battle for Quentin, I think, but one he had to fight. This was his first film, and he was being treated as a new, high-profile talent—which he was—that Hollywood was hot to embrace. And he came up against a force of nature that didn't care. It was a lesson, and made him a better director, as when he dealt with other actors later in his career. He'd been bloodied, but came out on the other side as a filmmaker who looked beyond his own words when shooting a scene. Quentin saw what Larry was, who he was, and truly wanted that element in his film, and it's the beating heart of *Reservoir Dogs*. But, he wasn't really ready for the fact that if you hire the real deal for a crime picture, the "real deal" is what you get.

Dogs, of course, was an enormous success, and Quentin sent me a postcard from Spain after he'd shown it to Sam Fuller. He was justifiably proud, loved Larry in the film, but talked about some of their problems in an interview, and said that it might have been better if he'd hired John Ireland. Big mistake. Larry was no fan of Ireland's, their bad-blood history went back to the 40s, and this comment really got under his skin, despite the fact that being in Quentin's movie was giving him new fans and helping with a glorious, final act to his career.

After Quentin's European jaunt, we were at Cathryn's, and wandered out to the sidewalk, and I told him about Larry's reaction to John Ireland. He was truly sorry about it and also understood. These men were the guys he wrote about. They were his characters, with the same codes of conduct. Larry stood in front of the *Dogs* camera, Ireland didn't, and that had to count for something. Quentin knew that better than anyone, and to his true credit, called Larry to apologize in one of the best birthday presents he could have given the old bull.

Quentin himself then went nuclear. Success followed success, with the Oscars stacking up. Some of the old Cathryn Jaymes circle still worked with him, some didn't, as his movies became something akin to a cultural phenomenon. Our times together, naturally, became more rare, but we always picked up with more movie history, and I felt good that Quentin would refer to me as a guy he could completely talk movies with, especially horror and Westerns. That much hadn't changed.

Our mutual love of Elmore Leonard resulted in his brilliantly adapting *Rum Punch* into *Jackie Brown*, and my loving it. It's actually my favorite film, because he so honored Leonard's prose and structure and wrote a stunning script from that book. Quentin let Leonard take front position on the film, and it was a modest, and excellent, artistic choice.

Much has gone on as the years have fallen away. I think the deaths of Cathryn and Quentin's long-time editor Sally Menke affected him deeply, and those feelings of loss have found their way into movies like *Inglourious Basterds*. His choices, and he has incredible freedom on all fronts, still reflect the movie fan, the guy who stays up until four in the morning to catch an old Steve Cochran flick.

That hasn't changed. While he became involved with the New Beverly Theater, making sure folks haven't forgotten Franco Nero or Terence Fisher, he's also turned his attention to Westerns, with great success that's pumped new energy into the genre.

When the Western Writers of America gave him their prestigious award for the script to *Django Unchained*, I was happy to accept it, and my mind was flashing back—not to those first days in Scott Spiegel's apartment—but to a few months before, when I got a call from Quentin one night, and we talked Westerns. He was getting ready to take a look at *Death of a Gunfighter*, starring Richard Widmark, and the first movie to carry the "Directed by Alan Smithee" credit, since neither Don Siegel or Robert Totten felt they should get full credit. It's a nice little movie, and the best "Smithee" film ever, and we talked about that. And John Wayne, and Sergio Corbucci, and Morricone, and on and on. For about an hour.

Maybe one day I'll get another call, or we'll grab a burger, and we'll pick up right where he left off, at the very thing that brought us together so many years ago, before all that's happened: the love of the movies, and no matter whatever happens, I know Quentin will never lose that.

INTRODUCTION: DO GO *HATEFUL* INTO THIS GOOD NIGHT
by Jason Pankoke

Chances are excellent that, whether you have picked up this book out of general curiosity or heightened interest, an introduction to the filmmaker Quentin Tarantino is hardly necessary. It does *not* mean that a refresher on the man who became the maverick behind the likes of *Pulp Fiction, Kill Bill Vol. 1* and *2*, and *Inglourious Basterds* is without merit. As author Andrew J. Rausch sets up in his opening statement and proves handily with the interview transcripts that follow, *Conversations on Quentin Tarantino* is a nifty companion to the analyses of Tarantino's life and work that already exist out there in the world.

So, why *another* tome on Tarantino to add to your reading pile or permanent collection? Consider that our subject, a movie director confident with visual storytelling technique and a screenwriter adept with poetically-verbose dialogue, is a vital force today after springing forth from the fabled American independent film movement of the 1990s. Recent hubbub over *The Hateful Eight*, his eighth "film proper" released nearly a quarter century after his debut *Reservoir Dogs*, is proof his distinctive voice and career still matter to many. He takes chances and hits way more than misses, not unlike his flawed-yet-personable protagonists.

In other words, much remains to be explored about one of the few big Hollywood directors not chained to the blockbuster assembly line whose work still turns heads as well as a profit. Whereas scholars, critics, and fanboys have picked apart his films and scripts in the attempt to identify his influences or obsessions, Rausch in *Conversations on Quentin Tarantino* lets the history speak for itself on how mild-mannered Tarantino the Video Store Clerk solidified his path into becoming Tarantino the Miramax-Weinstein Superstar. These interviews are not glorified rumor mills but *bona fide* first-person anecdotes shared in conversation by industry veterans.

Who, then, are the players cast by Rausch to embellish this wide-ranging tale? They are collaborators and coconspirators. They have verbally expounded on the wonder of the cinema with Tarantino and crawled through the Tinseltown trenches alongside Tarantino. For the most part, they are not the stars on the poster for "a film by Quentin Tarantino" but talented craftspeople who have worked on his features, spin-offs from his features, or licensed media based on his features such as the *Django Unchained* comic book series. From journalists to make-up gurus to cult film titans and more, they comprise the novel tapestry of *Conversations on Quentin Tarantino*.

It is satisfying to learn about the various ways these contemporaries past and present helped ensure the Tarantino we know today would emerge, reminding us that success on any level still "takes a village." Insider stories worth pointing out in this respect include those shared by Don Murphy, who produced a *Natural Born Killers* that differed from the screenplay sold by Tarantino, and Bill Unger and the late Tony Scott, who almost regretted entrusting a rewrite of *Crimson Tide* to Tarantino after bringing to fruition the young gun's original script, *True Romance*. We forget that Tarantino took his lumps and learned his lessons like everyone else.

It is also heartening to bask in the nostalgic glow of his early years as painted by former coworkers and customers, some of whom became his earliest partners in film, at the long-gone Video Archives in Los Angeles where he served as talkative clerk and walking encyclopedia. Rausch has done *Conversations on Quentin Tarantino* a great service by reaching this far back to recall those "on the cusp" Tarantino years. It humanizes the man and illustrates the relationship between his passions, quirks, and early projects—including the mythical first feature that wasn't (but really is), *My Best Friend's Birthday*—before "the biz" became instrumental to his growth.

My first Tarantino was his official second film, *Pulp Fiction*, which I did not see during its original 1994-5 release. I had plenty of opportunity, of course, living in a college town where this hipster favorite was held over for several months in a row. Not unlike with *The Blair Witch Project* a few years later, but for radically different reasons, friends wanted to tell me all about it but hesitated in order to preserve its surprises. I eventually rented a Japanese import Laserdisc of *Pulp Fiction* from our own local video emporium, That's Rentertainment, and highly enjoyed the narrative Tarantino puzzle that unfolded before my eyes and ears.

Not long afterwards, I would see both *Jackie Brown* at a film festival and the Hong Kong drama *City on Fire* at a nearby theater. I also received in the mail Mike White's ahead-of-its-time video criticism, *Who Do You Think You're Fooling?*, which compares side-by-side the sequences most similar in *Reservoir Dogs* and the five-years-older *City on Fire*. It was hard to ignore the saga as it unfurled in the media and specialty press. Could a filmmaker's influences get the best of a film? Does derivativeness equal bad or lazy storytelling? Would the writing Oscar won by Tarantino for *Pulp Fiction* encourage him to jump the chronological shark?

Five official films and many years later, those 1990s quandaries hold little water, as the maturing Tarantino *oeuvre* fascinates us still. Given his last three theatrical efforts have been violent period pieces, however, one wonders if his tendencies will continue to pass muster as our society leans towards increasingly puerile or politically-narrow entertainments. On the other hand, upcoming generations might rely on his stylistically-anachronistic work as a way to experience our film past in present-day form. No matter what, trust in Tarantino to please the fans and rankle others' nerves with his on-screen verve and off-screen panache as long as he can.

If you plan to belatedly catch up with Quentin Tarantino via *The Hateful Eight*, which will have been released to home video and streaming platforms by the time you read this, do yourselves a favor, or two, or three. Watch *Hateful* on the biggest screen and with the fullest of sound as possible. Then, scold yourself a little for not taking advantage of its theatrical or 70mm "roadshow" runs to best experience what Tarantino the Film Provocateur had in store for you, assuming you skipped out. Finally, lift your spirits back up by cracking open one more time *Conversations on Quentin Tarantino*, Andrew J. Rausch's long-gestating entry in a lively "film section" subgenre that can stand quite well on its own.

AUTHOR'S NOTE
by Andrew J. Rausch

I always loved film. Some of my earliest memories involve movies. I still remember watching Joe Camp's *Benji* as a young lad. Then I got a little bit older and I started attending the drive-in with my parents to see movies like *Smokey and the Bandit* and *Superman*. I wasn't a very discerning viewer back in those days. As a young man, I loved everything I watched, from *Salem's Lot* to lesser fare like *Porky's* and *Super Fuzz*.

It wasn't until October 14, 1994 that I began to see film more clearly. It was on that night—opening night—that I first saw Quentin Tarantino's *Pulp Fiction*. (I'll admit it, I still hadn't seen *Reservoir Dogs* at this point.) When that movie came blaring to life on the screen before me, complete with unbelievably-cool music from Kool and the Gang and Dick Dale, my eyes were forced opened for the first time. It was then that I truly came to realize everything that cinema could actually be. This was the first time I really considered that there was a man called a director behind this thing, pulling the strings like a talented puppet master. This movie would forever change my life.

Some time later, I was in Seattle, Washington, trying to convince this really cute girl that she should go on a date with me. We went to a bookstore (as "friends"), and I stumbled across two books that would almost have as significant an impact on me as that film had. They were *Quentin Tarantino: The Man and His Movies* by Jami Bernard and Jeff Dawson's *Quentin Tarantino: The Cinema of Cool*. These were the first books on the subject of cinema I would ever possess. And that night, when I went back to my hotel room alone and rejected by that cute girl, I didn't feel lonely or sad at all. I had those magnificent books to keep me company. And as I read the two biographies of this man Quentin Tarantino, I started to see the path before me in a new light. I had always planned on being a writer, but I never knew what I would write about. But here in my hands were exactly the types of books I wanted to write. On that night, I fell in love with film books and even more deeply in love with the works of Tarantino. That was when I came up with the idea that would eventually result in this book. What if I made a companion book to the films of Quentin Tarantino, rather than a biography? At that time there was no such book, and it seemed like a brilliant idea.

It was then that I embarked upon a journey which would stretch out over the next twenty years. I began researching Tarantino and interviewing anyone who knew him that I could get close to. But somehow the book stalled for a good long time after the release of *Jackie Brown*. I actually had the opportunity to have a really great conversation with Tarantino at the QTIII festival in Austin, Texas, about the merits of the under-appreciated film *Death Collector*, as well as the copious deficiencies found in the laughable Cannon musical *The Apple*. I would later have a similarly good time with *Pulp Fiction* co-writer Roger Avary, in which he detailed the even-longer theory he and Tarantino had conceived about *Top Gun* containing homosexual subtext.

But after that, the book started and stopped intermittently. My attentions were pulled towards a number of other projects. (I published nearly thirty books during that span, none of which were the Tarantino book.) And each time a new (and equally wonderful) Tarantino offering was unleashed upon the movie-going public, I would vow to finally finish my book. But I never did. Then I read Dale Sherman's terrific book *Quentin Tarantino F.A.Q.* and quickly realized he had crafted pretty much the same book I had always envisioned. So my dream of twenty years looked as though it were finally dead. Then, not long after the release of Tarantino's eighth "official" film, *The Hateful Eight*, I had a conversation with BearManor Media editor Ben Ohmart. It was in that discussion the book would find new life as a collection of original interviews on all things Tarantino.

And so, after two decades in the making, I present you with *Conversations on Quentin Tarantino*. I hope you enjoy reading it as much as I enjoyed putting it together.

JAMI BERNARD

Jami Bernard is an author and media consultant, as well as an award-winning film critic for *The New York Post* and *The New York Daily News*. She is also the founder of Barncat Publishing. She appeared in and was a consultant on the Independent Film Channel's Indie Sex series. She also penned a *Lois Lane* comic book for DC Comics, in which Lois was based on Bernard's early career at *The New York Post*. She has appeared frequently on such television programs as *Oprah* and *The Today Show* and has published in numerous publications, including *Entertainment Weekly, Seventeen, Glamour,* and *Self.*

Her books include *The Incredible Shrinking Critic, Chick Flicks, First Films,* and the seminal biography *Quentin Tarantino: The Man and His Movies.*

It has been suggested that many characters in Tarantino's screenplays are actually based to some degree on himself. As his biographer, what characters do you believe most resemble their creator, and in what aspects?

Hmmm. You know, it's easier to be the interviewer than the interviewee. [Laughs.] You know, I concentrated a lot in my book on the characters who were based on his friends. Some of those are very clear.

Would you like to touch on that a little bit?

The Eric Stoltz drug-addicted character, Lance, in *Pulp Fiction,* was, I think, somewhat based on one of Quentin's friends. But

Quentin . . . I'm trying to think of which characters would be him. The Christian Slater character in *True Romance* is obviously him, or the way he would like to be. It's sort of an idealized depiction of the way he sees himself. You know, the guy who's a little bit different, likes comic books, likes action movies, wants a girl to love him for his real self . . . and had trouble finding a girl who was interested in the same things that interested him. Someone who would not be afraid to take action to defend his woman or to beat up the drug dealers. I mean, in this case they all die. And I think that's a bit of an exaggeration, although obviously Quentin has been in fights and he was a bit of a scrapper when he was a teenager. So he does know how to fight, but I don't know how he would do against a gang of thugs with guns. But that character of all his characters is the one that's closest to him.

What do you see as being the biggest misconceptions about Tarantino's films?

I think the biggest misconception, or the most annoying misconception, is that he planted meaning in a lot of small details. Now I believe he thought out the details. They're not there by mistake, but I don't think he meant for people to be guessing what's in the briefcase in *Pulp Fiction*. I think he lifted that idea of the glowing briefcase from *Kiss Me Deadly*. I think he took little things he was interested in cinematically, and the kind of fan base he has are the kind of people who nitpick and want to know every little thing. I mean, you can find relationships among characters and you can find things that relate back to each other, but then I think people go overboard in thinking there was extra meaning packed into every moment. I really don't think he meant for that to happen at all.

What do you think Tarantino's influence on the film world has been thus far in his career?

His influence is very broadly felt. First of all, he gave hope to young filmmakers and people with the dreams of being a filmmaker and to people who either didn't or didn't want to continue their education. I don't know if that was a good thing or a bad thing. People started to think that if he could not go to college or even finish high school and he could be this famous, then they too can be this famous. So then you get all these people from film school or not from film school making little Tarantino rip-offs. But Quentin really does have a talent, and you can't just fake that. Now we just have these films where people talk about a lot of nothing, or they're betraying each other right and left. You know, it just doesn't ring the same as something like *Pulp Fiction* or *Reservoir Dogs*.

You interviewed Tarantino's long-lost father in Premiere *a few years ago. Could you tell me a little bit about that?*

I'd tried to track down Quentin's father for my book. I tried very hard to track him down, but I couldn't find him. And I discussed this with Quentin. You know, Quentin loved my book. We sat down and had dinner in Toronto and discussed this at length. I told him about all the attempts I had made to track down his biological father, and he didn't have any real comment about it at the time. I know it would have been a big deal for him if his father had been found, but he didn't think it was wrong of me to try to find as many people to talk about him as possible.

But the thing is, the father found me after the book came out. He contacted me by e-mail and offered me an interview, so I figured if I ever update the book I could include that. So I interviewed him, and I printed it in *Premiere* magazine. Before I printed it, I went over all the facts of the story with Quentin's mother, Connie, to make sure this was the guy. Then I told his mother and publicist Bumble Ward to alert him to the fact that this was going to be running so he'd be prepared because I thought it might be an emotional shock. He had about two months to prepare himself. But then when the story came out, I guess it was too much for him to see a picture of this guy talking about him as though he knew him. Quentin got really upset over the article, and I'm sure he still holds it against me.

LARRY BISHOP

Larry Bishop was born into show business royalty, the son of Rat Pack member Joey Bishop. At the age of eighteen, Bishop was a member of the improvisational comedy troupe known as the Session, which also included Richard Dreyfuss, Rob Reiner, and Albert Brooks. He made his acting debut in *Wild in the Streets* in 1968. He soon became a contract player with American International Pictures and became synonymous with the motorcycle movie genre. He is perhaps best known for the film *The Savage Seven*. He also appeared on numerous television series such as *Laverne & Shirley, Kung Fu,* and *I Dream of Jeannie.*

In 1996, he wrote and directed the film *Mad Dog Time*, which featured Ellen Barkin, Gabriel Byrne, and Richard Dreyfuss. That same year, he wrote and starred in the film *Underworld* alongside Denis Leary and Joe Mantegna. In 2004, he appeared in *Kill Bill: Vol. 2*. He later wrote, directed, and starred in the Quentin Tarantino-produced film *Hell Ride*.

When did you first become aware of Quentin Tarantino?

I became aware of Quentin when *Reservoir Dogs* opened. I brought my oldest son with me to the movie theater. He was in his late teens at the time. He had actually typed up some of my scripts, and he was really worried that *Reservoir Dogs* was going to affect what I was doing. He was a little bit worried that whoever this Quentin Tarantino guy was, it was going to affect me in my attempts to sell my own similar projects. I said, "No, let's just see the movie." So we went to see *Reservoir Dogs* at the Fine Arts

Theater in Beverly Hills. I remember it as if it was yesterday. There were twelve people in the audience for that movie. My son kept saying, "It's funny, it's violent, it's a lot like your stuff. Do you think this is going to get in your way?" I said, "Let's just relax and watch the movie. If the guy is talented, he's talented. What difference does it make? If he hits it big before my scripts hit it big, I'll just deal with it." But my son was very concerned.

I always sit in the back of the movie theater. Besides watching the movie, I want to see how people are responding to the material. We both really liked the movie, so that wasn't what was at stake. When we finally left the theater, my son said, "Well, it's funny and it's violent. There are real similarities." Then he said, "But there were only twelve people in the theater." I remember this very clearly. I never root against anybody who's got talent. I said, "Yeah, but we both really liked that movie." Besides that, I watched the audience. There were only twelve people in that theater other than us, and they were all guys, sitting separately. I said, "I got news for you—this Tarantino guy's gonna go places, because those twelve people were really engaged in watching that movie." I watched their body movements. They were really riveted. Nobody went to the bathroom, nobody got up for popcorn . . . Those twelve people were really engaged. So when I left that theater, I knew that Quentin had himself a career. I didn't know what kind of career he was going to wind up having, but I knew he wasn't going to have to work on any other kind of thing except movies. I knew he could do this for the rest of his life. It was actually exciting to see somebody who was that talented.

How did you wind up meeting Quentin?

What happened was, I got a phone call back in 2001. I got a call from my friend Laura Cayoutte at midnight. She said, "I'm standing next to Quentin Tarantino, and he's your biggest fan." That's the first thing she says to me. I assumed he was a fan because I had just done a bunch of gangster movies—*Mad Dog Time, Underworld*. . . . I said, "He really liked the gangster movies?" And she said, "No, no, no. He loves the motorcycle movies you did in the late sixties and early seventies. He loves

Savage Seven." So he got on the phone and he said, "Do you want to see a mint print of *Savage Seven*? Come to my house and we'll watch it in my theater." I said, "Yeah, when?" And he said, "Let's do it tomorrow night." So that was the beginning. That was like a real big kick, because no one in show business liked those motorcycle movies. *No one.*

In all of the time since—from 1967 to 2001—not one person had ever said a nice thing about the motorcycle movies. But he flipped for them. He loved *The Savage Seven*. It's one of his favorite movies, so he really got it. He liked the grindhouse movie ambiance. They were not part of the mainstream, which was what I liked about them. Because I had been raised in a Hollywood setting. Because of my father and the whole Rat Pack thing, I had been around show business from the time I was two. That was the top of the line in show business, with Frank Sinatra and Dean Martin. You couldn't get any bigger in show business than they were at that period. But that wasn't me. I liked rebel movies. I like Marlon Brando in *The Wild One*. I like James Dean in *Rebel Without a Cause*. In a way, they were the opposite of what I had been exposed to. I made a decision at nineteen that I was just going to make movies and wasn't going to do nightclubs. I wanted to separate myself from all the show business stuff I had experienced previously. The motorcycle movies weren't seen as a respected form of show business. But this was purposeful on my part. I didn't think it was a good thing, psychologically speaking, to follow very closely in the footsteps of my father. But no one had *ever* complimented me for those movies before. No one. So Quentin was completely separate from anybody I had ever met in show business. He appreciated those movies for what they were.

So Quentin said, "Come on up to my house." So I went to his house the following night. He's got a fifty-seat movie theater in his house, and it's beautiful. He's got a little lobby before you enter the movie theater, and he had posters of all my movies on display in his lobby! They used to tell you in the late sixties that if you ever took LSD, you'd have flashbacks later on. It was unpredictable. Well, that was the first thing that hit my brain, because my brain started to go very surreal on me. It was so unusual, just totally unexpected. So my first thought was, *Uh-oh, they were right.* This was the acid kicking in from forty years ago. [Laughs.] My first thought was, *Are these posters always in his lobby? Or did he do this for me?* Either way, it was like *wow, he's really doing this.* This was really generous of spirit.

Then when we got into the movie theater, he said, "You're in for a surprise now." Before *The Savage Seven* started running, he had seven trailers of my films put together. I hadn't even seen these trailers. He had put them together. I said, "I know there's no official Larry Bishop package of trailers. How did you do this? Where did you get all of these?" And he said, "Just sit back and enjoy the movie." So I still don't know why I'm up there outside of the joy I'm getting. The movie ends, the lights come up, and I thank him. I said, "So what do you want to do?" I knew there had to be something else he wanted to say to me. And he said, "I think it's your destiny to write, star, and direct the greatest motorcycle movie ever made." That was his line—that it was my destiny to do that. So I said, "I'm in." And that's how *Hell Ride* began.

So I started writing, and about a week later he said, "I wrote a part for you in *Kill Bill*." I said, "Of course, I'll do it." I didn't even ask him what the part was. He just said my character was someone who was going to give Michael Madsen's character a very, very, very hard time. "You're gonna be totally sadistic with him. You're gonna cut him off at the knees." So I said, "Perfect."

What was the experience of working on Kill Bill *like?*

It was fantastic. First of all, I didn't know he was going to call the part "Larry." That was really interesting to me. That excited me. There wasn't going to be any doubt in anybody's mind that he really wrote that part for me. That was exciting.

We never talked about the role, Quentin and I, because he went off to travel all over the world making this movie. We never said anything about the scene one way or the other. The only communication we had was through the wardrobe people. They told me, "Quentin said, 'Bring your clothes.' We're not giving Larry clothes. I want him to go into his closet and wear the clothes that he always wears." That was cool. So when I showed up the first day, this was the first time we ever said anything. He said, "Why don't we have a run-through? Not for the blocking, but let's just go through it." So it was just me and Michael Madsen going back and forth with the dialogue. When we did it the first time, I had a very specific idea of what I wanted to do. And Quentin says, "That wasn't exactly what I thought you were gonna do." He wanted urban New York fast-speak, which is what I do. But for me, I thought I had to slow things down for this character. I knew I was going to play it with a lot of ego. I felt like in his world, he's like Frank Sinatra. This is his world, where he's as big as Frank Sinatra. I wanted to express that.

So instead of rushing into the dialogue, I just held for twelve seconds looking at Michael Madsen. I felt like it would be more uncomfortable for Madsen's character for me to just stare at him. It's a sadistic move. It's cruel to do it. But I felt like it sets the tone for the power dynamic we're working on. So every time Quentin said "action," I hold for twelve seconds. And Quentin held for twelve seconds on the cut! I didn't think he'd do that, but I knew he'd understand where my mindset was at. I felt that was important. I figure there's no way in the world he's going to use all that when he puts this together, or maybe he'll use a couple of seconds. But he used every single bit of it. And Quentin told me, "You know how to hold those pauses." That was really cool to me. I mean, I wondered, could my presence hold those pauses? It's always a little bit of a gamble.

After we did that, Michael Madsen walks over to me and said, "Larry, the scene's all yours." That was a pretty generous thing to say. So I was thinking of him for *Hell Ride*, but now he had consolidated it. I found him to be a compatriot of mine. Even though we could have conflicts on *Hell Ride*, I wanted him to be on my side. I figured a biker would appreciate someone backing them like that. That was an unusual thing for an actor to say. But I think the more I dug in with how I wanted to play the part, the better it was for Michael. I think it's a great scene for him. We know his character's background—he could cut off my head in a second. But no, he's gonna take it. There's a reason he's gonna take it. If you watch the movie a couple of times, I think it benefited him. I wasn't taking the scene away from him, I was enhancing a different way of looking at his character.

Also cool, Robert Richardson, the cinematographer, turns to Quentin Tarantino and says, "Who the fuck is this guy?" He knows nothing about me, except that he can't get over what he just saw. He was sort of watching it just to get a sense of the lighting and the coverage, but he said, "Who the fuck is this guy?" That tickled Quentin. I didn't want to interrupt him because it was so beautiful; he went on for ten minutes about who I was. Robert Richardson knew absolutely nothing about me but what he'd just seen.

In the movie, I say, "That fucking hat." That was like code words for everybody. That went on for the rest of the shoot. Everybody was saying, "That fucking hat." That wasn't in the original script. When I got there, Quentin handed me three handwritten pages. He said, "I've got to get Michael Madsen to take this fucking hat off. He won't stop wearing that hat in the movie. So you're gonna be the one who tells him to take the fucking hat off." So that was the inside joke of the whole thing. "Let's get Michael's hat off." And the handwritten pages, I took that idea later on. When I went to do *Hell Ride*, I thought it was beneficial that the director took the time to write these extra things in his handwriting. It made me have a different feeling when I was looking at the pages. I never forgot that. So I did that myself during *Hell Ride*. I think it changes the tenor of the way you see things as an actor.

Working on *Kill Bill* set the tone for how much I trusted Quentin when I worked with him. It couldn't have worked out better. Even to this day, when I'm at a newsstand or Rite-Aid, there's always somebody who's staring at me. I've gotten to the point where I can recognize a *Kill Bill* look. I get different looks for different movies. But this one was out there, and it plays everyday on cable. There could be a *Kill Bill* channel as much as it plays! I get that kind of attention all the time because of this movie.

What was Quentin like to work with on Hell Ride?

He was a doll. We had two meetings at the very beginning,

just to make sure we were both on the same page. I said, "What do you think I should call my character?" So I let him anoint me with the name. He said, "Pistolero is a good name for you." So I said, "Perfect. I'll be Pistolero." We were in sync on all this. We both loved Sergio Leone, and that's where the humor and the violence came into play in both of our films. Quentin and I have different senses of humor, but it's a strong sense of humor. I knew we were making a biker movie with kind of a Spaghetti Western vibe going on. That was our meeting point in terms of what we were going to do. I was happy to see that everything I wrote wound up in the movie.

Here's what Quentin did. He was going to leave me completely alone during the shoot, which was very cool. The last thing he said to me after our second meeting was, "I'll see you in the editing room." That was it. So I went off to make the movie, and then went into the editing room. He came in for about three weeks after I did my cut. He was brilliant.

I had written the script so graphically that when I had made the deal with the Weinsteins, Bob said, "What kind of rating are we gonna get on this?" I said, "I'll get you an R-rating." He felt that it was written so graphically that it wouldn't even get an NC-17. They were going to have to invent something for us. But I said, "No, I'll get you the R-rating." And that was the end of the issue. When we were going to the motion pictures ratings board, everyone was sending me notes for what to say when it didn't get the R-rating. There was pages of this stuff. But we passed on the first screening. Everybody kind of fainted. It was really crazy, but it was really Quentin. He knew how to get an R-rating. He knew how to do it without hurting what I was interested in—the eroticism mostly. I felt that was important to the picture.

PAUL CALDERON

Puerto Rican thespian Paul Calderon is a founding member of the Touchstone Theatre, the American Folk Theatre, and the LAByrinth Theater Company. A veteran of the stage, Calderon made his TV debut on the soap opera *As the World Turns*. In 1985, he made his screen debut in the film *Tenement*. He then appeared on a number of television series, such as *Miami Vice* (playing three different characters) and *The Equalizer*. He was a drug dealer in the Martin Scorsese-helmed Michael Jackson video "Bad." He has since maintained a very avid acting career and has appeared in such notable films as *Sea of Love, King of New York,* and *Bad Lieutenant*, which he also co-wrote.

In 1993, he was cast in Quentin Tarantino's second film, *Pulp Fiction*. He was initially up for the role of Jules Winnfield, but eventually lost out to Samuel L. Jackson. Tarantino then cast him as bartender English Bob. ("My name is Paul, this is between y'all.") Two years later, Calderon worked with Tarantino again on the anthology film *Four Rooms*, acting alongside Bruce Willis, Tim Roth, Quentin Tarantino, and Jennifer Beals.

The versatile actor has since worked on such films as *Kiss of Death, Cop Land,* and *21 Grams*, as well as made a handful of appearances on the various *Law & Order* series.

You were originally slated to play Jules in Pulp Fiction. *How did all that go down?*

I got a call from my agent. He said, "There's this filmmaker named Quentin Tarantino, and he's interested in you for his new film called *Pulp Fiction*." I hadn't seen *Reservoir Dogs* yet, but I had heard about it. So they sent me the script. I read it, and they said they wanted to see me for the character of Jules. I went down to the Tribeca film area, and Lawrence Bender, the producer, was there. Quentin was there, too. He said he was a big fan of mine and had seen me in *King of New York* and *Q&A*. He said, "Can you read for this?" You know, back then we didn't have video cameras to record anything. So I said, "Sure." I had connected with the character—the rhythm of the language. I read and there was a look between Quentin and Lawrence. He said, "Can you read the other scenes?" So I auditioned, and at the end of my audition, Quentin started applauding. It's the only time in my career that someone applauded during an audition. [Laughs.] I noticed that Lawrence did this weird thing. He got up on his chair and sat on the back of the chair. Quentin said, "You know, originally I had you in mind for this role English Bob," which is the role I wound up playing in the film anyway. He said he had written that character with me in mind. He said, "Let's put that aside for now and you'll hear from me."

A couple of weeks passed and I didn't hear anything back. Then I started reading in the newspaper that there was some stuff going on. Then my agent told me there were some legal ramifications, blah, blah, blah, blah, blah. And then a month later, I was called in to L.A. to audition again. Sam Jackson and I were both going to audition at the Culver studios. It was on a weekend, and there was nobody there, except the producers and the casting agents. Quentin was a little bit late. I got there first, and they were seeing me before Sam. I later found out from Sam that there was some sort of legal agreement that he was going to play the part, and then he didn't do that well when Quentin brought him in to read. He didn't know there was going to be an audition, so he didn't try that hard. It was something of that nature, which I don't discount. So Quentin arrives late and I audition, and it just didn't go that well. The casting director said I did really, really well, but I didn't nail it the way I had nailed it back in New York. I just felt deflated by the audition. Out in the parking lot, I'm waiting for my ride to arrive and Quentin's exiting the building to have lunch before Sam arrives. He sees that I'm a little bit deflated, and he pats me on the back and gives me a thumbs up. And that was the last I saw of Quentin before I was on the set again. But I intuitively knew I didn't have the role. My plan was initially to stay in L.A. for a couple of weeks and meet people for some things, but I just took the night owl back to New York. Then the next day my agent confirmed it and said, "It didn't go your way." So I said, "Fine."

Then Quentin called me and asked if I would play the other role. I said, "Fine," and I did it. It was cool, just being on the set with everyone. Then he asked me later on to be in this film *Four Rooms*, and I did that. But Sam deserved it. He'd been working for a really long time, and he'd gone through a lot of ups and downs in his career. It just went his way, and that's the way it goes. Sometimes you only get an opportunity like that once. It's like pitching a perfect game—an error will fuck it up for you. It's fine. I'd be in a different place right now had that happened. I wouldn't be with my family right now. My oldest son was born the year after. I decided on that plane ride home, "Fuck it, I'm just gonna have a family." [Laughs.] We had two boys. One is twenty-one and one is nineteen. So that's what happened. Had that happened, my life would have gone a different route. It was that fork in the road where you have to decide which way you're going to go. I went the other way, and I have two great sons, and I have a beautiful wife I've been with since acting school back in 1977.

What was it like on the Pulp Fiction *set?*

It was cool. Quentin always provides a cool, open atmosphere. He's very genuine. He's very open with his actors, and he considers himself an actor. I had known Sam from New York. We had done several films together before he became a star. I knew Ving Rhames, as well. We were in a play together when he was twenty-three back in New York. Bruce was cool. Travolta was kind of quiet. It was a cool set.

I remember Quentin telling me, "You just missed Sonny Chiba. He was here on the set." [Laughs.] Sonny Chiba—the Japanese actor. I was like, "No, please don't tell me that!" But it was cool.

We did movie trivia. We would just quiz each other about films. It was a good set; a nice set. Very cool.

From an actor's standpoint, what does Quentin Tarantino give you that's helpful in regards to process?

He gives you a lot of respect. Because he is an actor himself, he doesn't call out suggestions or adjustments where everyone can hear. He would put his arm around you and you'd walk into a corner and he'd give you private adjustments. That way, no one but you knew what the adjustment was. So as an actor you know if you fuck up the adjustment, no one else will know except you and him. You don't have that pressure. And he respects you, and he respects the crew. You feel like you're in good hands and that he understands the process. You feel supported by him, and that's huge because many times you see directors who see you as an automaton; they just call out directions like you're a robot. But not Quentin. He respects the process.

Did you have any idea going into that just how big Pulp Fiction *was going to be?*

No. I knew it was gonna be a cool film, but I had no idea it was going to become the film that it became. It's like the *Gone with the Wind* of crime films, you know?

Do many fans come up to you and quote that "My name is Paul" line to you?

All the time. [Laughs.] That was improvised, you know. That wasn't even written. Quentin was like, "Hey, why don't you say this line? I think it'd be cool." I was like, "Sure." Just recently someone told me it was the coolest line in the film. They were still quoting it. I wish I could take credit for that line, but that was all Quentin. I don't know why people always quote that line. [Laughs again.] And I'm not taking credit for it. I think it's just that rhythm that Quentin writes in, and people just ride along to that rhythm. He basically creates songs for the audience to listen to. It's like quoting great lyrics. It's not so much the singer as it is the songwriting itself.

The character was named English Bob. Did Quentin tell you anything about the origin of that?

He told me, "I wrote this part specifically for you because you're always so cool and so sophisticated in your roles." He said the name just came to him, but he wrote it with me in mind.

What was it like working on Four Rooms?

That was crazy. My first son was born, and he was like eight weeks old when we flew out to do it. Quentin had called me. He said, "I wrote this cool part. Would you read it and tell me whether you want to do it or not?" I said, "No matter what you wrote, I'll do it." He said, "No, read it first and then call me and let me know." It was cool. It was based on "The Man from Rio" from *Alfred Hitchcock Presents*. It was based on a short story and it had Peter Lorrie and Steve McQueen originating those roles. [Laughs.] I read it and I said, "You ripped this off from Alfred Hitchcock." He laughed and said, "Yeah, I did. I wanted to pay homage to them."

Bruce was great to work with. Very inventive. Quentin as an actor is very inventive. It was cool to work with a director who was also one of the lead actors. It was just a lot of fun.

Have you had any contact with Quentin since those films?

No, man. The last time I saw him I was out in LA. I was doing ADR [Automated Dialogue Replacement] for *Four Rooms*. The thing with Quentin is, he falls in love with actors. It's like someone who has affairs. He just falls in love with a lot of different actors, and he wants to use them. You can't hold it against him. I mean, a part of you says, "Hey, how about me? You said we were gonna work together again." But you know, directors are like that. They become infatuated with different actors and their quirks, and for a time being you're on their radar. Then you fall off.

OMAR DOOM

Omar Doom is an actor, director, musician, and artist. After meeting Quentin Tarantino, the filmmaker convinced him to shorten his birth name ("Omar Makhdomi") to the shorter stage pseudonym. The *Reservoir Dogs* helmer also persuaded the young musician to consider acting. "Quentin told me I'd be great in movies," Doom would later say in a press junket. "He really pushed me. I decided to go for it. I took his advice and I studied acting." This would ultimately pay off for the would-be actor, who landed his first role in Tarantino's *Death Proof* as Vanessa Ferlito's love interest. Tarantino would later cast Doom a second time as Private First Class Omar Ulmer in *Inglourious Basterds*.

Tarantino and Doom remain good friends, and Tarantino often invites him to his home for movie marathons. One year Tarantino threw the actor a birthday party in which he screened cartoons and movies, including *Hammerhead* and *The Mack*.

When did you first meet Quentin Tarantino?

We met through mutual friends around 1998.

Were you a fan of his work prior to meeting him? Did he influence you as a filmmaker?

I was and have always been a huge fan of his work. I still watch his movies pretty regularly. Everything I've learned about making movies I learned from watching him work. You'll be able to see what I come up with in the near future.

I understand that Quentin actually came up with your stage name, "Omar Doom." Tell me about that.

When I was twenty-three, I was having lunch with Quentin at the restaurant Toi on Sunset in Hollywood. I was telling him that I was thinking of shortening my name from Omar Makhdomi to Omar Makhdom. He said, "Why not just be Omar Doom?" I had never thought of that, and at first I thought it was a little too ridiculous, but after a while I was convinced. I was like, "Fuck it, I'm gonna do it." And I've never regretted it.

What do you see as being Quentin's biggest strengths in terms of directing?

People normally praise him for his writing, but I think he is also a phenomenal director. He has a very artistic way of blocking his scenes and framing his shots. As with everything he does, he shatters any rules or conventions. Also, he has very strong convictions. He was so adamant about doing real non-CGI high speed car chases in *Death Proof* that he built a supercharged camera truck that he sat in, driving over a hundred miles an hour to get those amazing shots.

What's the most interesting conversation you've ever had with him?

That's a hard one, because there are so many. I don't know which is the best, but one that stands out in my mind was about his meeting Bob Dylan. Apparently Bob Dylan boxes and has his own boxing ring. And Quentin and Bob Dylan actually boxed. The thought of that happening just blows my mind.

How did you become involved with Death Proof?

I got ahold of the script and basically begged him to read for it. He may have already been planning to bring me into the fold, but I didn't waste any time making sure it happened.

What were your thoughts on the script the first time you read it?

It was like reading any of his scripts for the first time. They're always read in one sitting because they're just impossible to put down. And the endings always make the hairs on my arms stick straight up and I get chills down my neck. But with *Death Proof* in particular, knowing that he names characters after his close friends, and then seeing that he'd named a character Omar was just an incredible thing. I was basically in the movie before I was in the movie.

What was that cast like to work with?

We were mostly all the same age on that set, so we hung out a lot. I made some lifelong friendships on that movie. That doesn't usually happen on movie sets. But something about Quentin's sets makes it really feel like everyone is part of a big family. There's no set like a Tarantino set. Everyone knows that the next movie set experience you have after working on a Tarantino movie is gonna suck, no matter what the movie is. Quentin told me that himself. Except it turned out that he was all wrong because my next movie ended up being *Inglourious Basterds*. I remember asking Quentin, "Remember telling me my next job was gonna suck? You were wrong."

I've heard that he screens movies for the cast and crew sometimes. Did he do this on the two movies you worked on, and if so, what were some of those films?

Usually they have something to do with whatever we're shooting or the actors we're working with. For example, during *Death Proof* we watched *Used Cars* with Kurt Russell. That was quite an experience. Kurt got a real kick out of that, just as we all did.

What was Kurt Russell like to work with?

He's a very humble guy who, like the rest of us, really felt that working with Quentin is just really something special. He didn't treat it like it was just one of the hundreds of movies he's worked on. For me personally, as a big fan of his work, it was an absolute joy just to be around him.

You worked pretty closely with Eli Roth on that picture. What's he like?

I worked on both *Death Proof* and *Inglourious Basterds* with Eli Roth, so we had already become friends. He's a great guy. Before meeting him, I saw *Hostel* with Quentin opening night in New York City, and I was just blown away. It's such a fun movie. Eli and I have a lot of similar interests film-wise. We both love a lot of the same horror/Giallo films, and he has introduced me to some great ones I had never seen. Eli and the rest of the Basterds all formed a brotherhood on that picture. We would all hang out on and off the set. It was a great time. Filming *Basterds* in Berlin is one of my fondest memories.

What are your thoughts on the final film Death Proof?

I love *Death Proof*. Quentin can pull off any genre, and it was a real treat to see his take on grindhouse horror/car chase films. I don't think anyone could have done it better. People have very short attention spans, so they weren't really ready for such a long double feature in theaters. But it's become a cult favorite since then. I get recognized a lot for that movie even though my role wasn't all that big.

How did you end up working on Inglourious Basterds?

I didn't go through the same audition process as I did for *Death Proof* on *Basterds*. Quentin just called me two weeks before I got on the plane and gave me an enthusiastic and bloody description of what I'd be doing—that I would be scalping and slaughtering Nazis left and right with Brad Pitt. He finished by saying, "Basically I want you to come to Berlin and be a Basterd." I just said, "Quentin, I've been preparing for this role my entire life."

What was working with Brad Pitt like?

Brad Pitt is a great example of how actors should conduct themselves. He's the chillest, most humble actor I've ever worked with. Some of the other big names showed up with a thick entourage of men in suits, while Brad just showed up with a six pack for the Basterds, saying, "You guys want a beer?" He was very encouraging to me during a lot of scenes with him, telling me that I had really come into my own throughout the film. It meant a lot to me. I hope I get to work with him again sometime.

Were you at all nervous going in to act in a big film like Basterds, *where you'd be working alongside so many talented performers?*

I actually wasn't. Working on *Basterds* was a pure joy. I was excited to get up and go to the set every day. Even when I was working in front of three or four hundred people, it was nothing but fun. Something about the way that Quentin works makes acting for him easy and such a thrill.

You were quite good in that film. Do people come up to you and recognize you from Inglourious Basterds?

I do get recognized for *Basterds* more than anything else. People ask me to do the Italian hand gesture for a picture, or say the Dominic DiCocco line. Depending on how many drinks I've had, I just might do it. I'm more proud of the work I did on that film than on anything else in my life, so it's nice to be recognized for it.

What was your favorite scene on that film, and why?

Busting through the door and killing Hitler and Gobbels with Eli would have to be my favorite day on set. When is someone ever going to have a chance to say they killed Hitler? In a Tarantino movie, no less! Well, I can now. I feel like I should make a business card that says "OMAR DOOM. I KILLED HITLER."

R.M. GUERA

R.M. Guera is a Serbian-born comic book author and illustrator who resides in Barcelona, Spain. He broke into the comic book industry in 1982 with the Spaghetti Western comic *Elmer Jones*. He further solidified his reputation as a go-to Western illustrator in the 1984 comic *Texas Riders*. However, it wasn't until Guera worked on the critically-acclaimed Vertigo series *Scalped* that he really became a star in the comic book world.

In 2012, he was handpicked to illustrate the Quentin Tarantino adaptation series *Django Unchained*. Tarantino, a huge comic book fan, could hardly contain his enthusiasm regarding the series. "One of the things that I'm really excited about is that *Django Unchained* is a big epic," Tarantino said. "When I write big epic scripts like *Kill Bill*, there's a lot of stuff that doesn't make the movie because they're too fucking big. They'd be four-hour movies if I did everything that was in the script, so there always is this aspect that the script is this big literary piece that I'm always taking it out and changing it and transforming it to make it a movie by the time it's all finished. That's the process: I'm always adapting my movie every day, my unwieldy script into a movie every day as I do it, but what's really cool about doing a *Django Unchained* comic book is that it's the entire script. Even though things might have changed in the movie, I might have changed something else, I might have dropped chapters, I might have dropped big pieces—now that will all be in the comic. The comic will literally be that very first draft of the script. All that material that didn't make the movie, all of that will be part of the piece. And I'm really excited about it."

How did you become involved with the Django Unchained *project?*

Back in 2009, I did a short comic on one *Inglourious Basterds* sequence from Tarantino's script. Rob Wilson from *Playboy* offered it to me. He sent me a very nice mail. The base for their offer was my art on *Scalped*. I must say, at that time for me it was out of the blue, as the only celebrity that I knew liked it was Samuel L. Jackson, as he said it on some talk show.

I did do it. It later was included in the special edition of the DVD, so it looks like Quentin liked the whole thing. Somewhere around July or August of last year, Ben Albernathy from DC contacted me about doing a *Django* comic book based on the completed first draft of the movie. Mail was even more flattering than the first time, and the terms and the script were really good. Two things are deep inside my drawing vein, and that's thinking visually in black-and-white and Western. Sometimes I think I saw all of that that were ever made. I grew up on black-and-white and Westerns. Everything I do is just closer or further from these two things. It's something like first impulse. So I of course accepted.

What were your initial thoughts when you read Tarantino's script for the first time?

It was a great script. They do seem to talk a lot, and for a comic book that can be a problem, but you definitely don't have the feel of words badly spent or dialogue wasted anywhere. Also, there are dynamics to the dialogue, so I could adapt it to panels more naturally. In comics, you have to work differently in showing background or ambiance, so dialogue flow has to catch its rhythm without using sound, obviously. I opted for establishing shots mostly while dialogue is going on, so the price for ease along reading is sometimes less effectiveness on humor or point made.

What's great is that there is subtle, though very, very constant, aim to all of them. Tarantino has this unusual charm of the story revealed in a somewhat different way, so once you catch the rhythm of that, it really is a joy to try to bring it to life. Simply put, you know where you're going. It's easier to create.

It's also nice when your initial feel for material can stay constant. Sometimes it happens that the fine point of the idea develops. Here, the equilibrium between complex and simple is just right.

What were some of the challenges you faced in crafting this series?

None as specific craft to use. I'm having some great time, really, but adaptation is time consuming, as the script is pretty thickly imagined for movie logic. Fast-paced dialogue is one thing in movies, and totally another in comics. Translation could be the word. It's like translating a poem; words are a tool, but the poetry of them is the real task.

With your creating different and unique looks for the characters outside the world of the movie, it's almost like you're directing your own version of Tarantino's script. Would you comment on that?

Thank you, sir. When I give master class sessions, one of the first things I tend to say is that the comic book artist's real job isn't to illustrate, but to express. There's a big difference, and not present enough on the comics scene. It is natural state, maybe the only one that's honest to use, to work on what emotionally justifies script. It's the same as actors with their acting roles: to feel them, and feel with them. In art, feel it first, you know? It is afterwards that one should use storytelling skills—not before.

Actual main cast is also not literally done. Common sense says not to go too far from what the movie already has, as it would simply be too much. But I did go towards what I think the actors themselves eventually wanted.

Technically, it is not a problem at all to just go portraying them as actors in their particular role. But I opted for sense of direction instead of just copying them. Even Christoph Waltz's Doc Schultz is done as half-tribute to the first *Django*, Italian actor Franco Nero. I tried to mingle in some elements of Nero's face along with Waltz's, and as with others, I'm leaving it to grow in naturally, by drawing them lots of times, and in lots of moods. So they visually become who they really are in my own interpretation. It's a fun time for me.

What has Quentin Tarantino's response to the comic been? I would have to think it's thrilling for him, as a comic book fan, to see his work immortalized in this fashion.

Thanks, it's nice of you to put it that way.

Technically, I have to say great, as I'm given the green light to anything I'd like to try or do. I'm very grateful for that. But it's a bit unusual experience, as I still couldn't communicate anything directly, although I had few, to me, mattering questions, especially about the story. I received through channels superlatives about my work, instead of answers. So in a way it is okay, but it's just plain strange considering the level we're eventually about.

I, in fact, don't know what Quentin thinks. That's the best answer I have to give. In practice, what's for sure is that I've again been lucky with editor Jim Chedwick. He is really superb, both as a person and as a professional.

Who do you consider your biggest artistic influences?

Basically all are old guys, and there's a lot of them. They came in waves by the age I was in. Most people wouldn't know who they are. . . .

The biggest influence ever—the one who made my bones—was Joao Mottini. All the rest would be muscle building on that. Too few people would know who he was, but amongst those who do, a certain look on the face is bound to appear, a sign of knowing he was something tremendous. The mold broke after that man. What I like most is that you start understanding his level best while you read. In context, not separately. He worked Westerns for a pretty short run—some three, maybe four years for UK's Fleetway. Then along came Alberto Breccia and Ruggero Giovannini, both leaving very strong ink statements in me.

From the U.S., there was Noel Sickles, Frank Robbins, Jack Davis. As I said, old guys. Finally, with my adolescence ending, there was Jean "Moebius" Giraud and Andre Franquin from France and Belgium, respectively. Also, although not influencing directly, Hugo Pratt leaves something very special in any artist's soul. His

Macumba for Gringo is just unforgettably-elevating stuff, like you're on something very strong.

Around the mid-seventies, I stopped caring about any actuality or masters [degree]. Books, movies, and long walks with long talks came—philosophy and questions. So, more in my life than my career, music, movies, and books mattered a lot. [Sam] Peckinpah, [Bob] Dylan, the blues in general, expressive guitars, Joseph Conrad—that kind of stuff. I'm still onto all that with people like Cormac McCarthy, T.P. Anderson, Bill Frisell. Almost any kind of pure transcendence in action, strong or nuanced, crude or sophisticated, all interests me. Not religion, though. I don't get along with that. To me, it lacks purity towards life.

Where do you go from here?

Work. I really enjoy working. Less resting from it. In fact, all one has is the moment you're working on something you love. Before and after is someone else's.

After *Django*, I have a very exciting new project scripted by the incredible Jason Aaron, the better half of our *Scalped* kid. The publisher is American, but still not set in stone; on the side there'll be a *Judge Dredd* short for the U.K.'s *2000AD*. There will be covers and maybe something more for Marvel. Overseas, by the end of the year, the book *Empire of the Steppes* for the French Delcourt. There's also an eventual sequel of my own pirate serial *Under the Shadowlight*, and the start of a new five-book story *Blues for Minnie*, both scripted by me, and both most probably for French Urban Comics.

The only detail is I'd maybe need two life times to do all I'm on to. So work is a pretty nice word.

SID HAIG

Sid Haig's first acting gig was in Jack Hill's UCLA student film *The Host*. This appearance launched a lengthy and eclectic acting career spanning more than four decades. Haig became a regular in Hill's films, including *Spider Baby*, *Coffy*, and *Foxy Brown*. Haig was also a regular player for producer Roger Corman. He also appears in George Lucas' *THX 1138* and the James Bond actioner *Diamonds Are Forever*. His many, many television appearances include such notable titles as *Batman*, *Charlie's Angels*, *Gunsmoke*, *Mission: Impossible*, *The A-Team*, and *The Dukes of Hazzard*. Haig's career has been resurrected as Captain Spaulding in filmmaker Rob Zombie's *House of 1,000 Corpses* and *The Devil's Rejects*.

After a brief retirement in 1992, Haig was offered the role of Marsellus Wallace in Quentin Tarantino's *Pulp Fiction*. However, he passed on the role; a decision he has since come to regret. Tarantino has since written roles specifically for the actor in both *Jackie Brown* and *Kill Bill*.

How did you meet Quentin Tarantino?

We actually met on an interview for *Pulp Fiction*. And that was the first time. I went in to read for Marsellus Wallace. Quentin said, "I've always enjoyed your work." I said, "Well, thank you. It's good to know that people are paying attention." And he goes, "Look around." I looked around the office and there were like six one-sheets from films I had done. He made me sign one before I left. So I did the audition and he wanted me to come back, and so I did the callback. He really wanted me to do it, and I really wanted to do it. In the process, the deal memo was offered, and it was for one day. I had told my agents I didn't want to do anything that even remotely looked like television because I had done so much, and television is not a creative medium. You put on the face, you say the words, don't bump into the furniture, and you get the job done. There were four locations involved. I said, "There are four locations here, and we're going to do this in a single day? That's like television." No one bothered to tell me Quentin doesn't work like that. It takes as long as it takes. So I turned it down because no one gave me the proper information. It's something I have regretted ever since because I could have had such a good time doing that, and Quentin was so cool that it was a major disappointment to me. I don't know how he felt about it. For that stupid little reason of non-communication. . . .

We worked together a couple more times. He called my house one day. I don't know how he got my number. I guess when you're Quentin Tarantino, you're like the CIA. You can get numbers from anywhere. But he called and he said, "I get that you don't want to do anymore stupid heavies and all that, but I've written a part for you. It's a judge. And you will play it. That's it. I won't take no for an answer." I said, "Okay, boss, whatever, let's go." That was for *Jackie Brown*. The thing that was cool was that he didn't tell Pam Grier that he had cast me in that role. So when she showed up on set, she just cracked up. We had done five pictures together, and *Jackie Brown* was our sixth. That was a good reunion. That was a one-day gig and I knew it was a one-day gig, and he got so much coverage and everything that it was just a really great thing.

What's it like as an actor working for Quentin Tarantino?

It's great because he's one of those few people that makes his vision clear to you and then gets out of the way and lets you do your job. He's done his job. He lets you do yours. If there's something that needs tweaked, fine, it gets tweaked, but he's not a puppet master, which most actors appreciate. In June, I will have been doing this for forty-nine years. I have an inkling what it takes to get the job done. I appreciate it when I run into a director like Quentin who lets you do it.

What was it like reuniting with Pam Grier on Jackie Brown?

See if I can expound on that. It was great. We had not seen each other in twenty-seven years. She showed up on the set, and it was like we'd just had lunch the day before. The relationship just picked right back up where we started. We had a great time. We had lunch together and did a lot of catching up. She was like my little sister. Working in the Philippines together for so long—you become very supportive of one another. You just kind of have to do that to survive, you know? When you're working in adverse conditions, tramping around in the jungle and watching out for snakes and spiders the size of dinner plates. You do stuff like that, you form a bond. You help each other get through. That's where we were, and it just picked right back up. I'm so happy that was a big success for her and got her moving to a higher level. That was great.

How did you become involved with Kill Bill?

There again, Quentin decided he wanted to have me in the film. That was kind of crazy because by the time I got on the film, the character I played, the bartender, was the fifth character I was assigned to. Originally, I was supposed to play the orderly at the beginning of the film. Then that got switched to something, and then that got switched to something else, and blah, blah, blah, back and forth until, finally, I ended up doing what I did. It was good.

Do you have any interesting stories about working on those films?

Yeah. This proves how much a film buff Quentin Tarantino is. He has truly dedicated himself to film. When I was on the set of *Jackie Brown*, he spent the day quoting every line from any film I ever did. Stuff that I had forgotten about, he remembered. He's got this mind that just captures everything. It was a kick. I went,

"Quentin, what the hell? Where are you pulling this stuff from?" He was like, "I remember I was sitting. . . ." "Okay, good." It was wild. And then when we did *Kill Bill*, there was a little kind of improvisational thing to open the whole thing up before Michael Madsen came into the scene. Because he knows that I do improvisational stuff, and he kind of wound me up and let me go. That was cool. That actually happened the first time, as a matter of fact, in *Jackie Brown* because I mispronounced Michael Keaton's character name. Michael corrected me. I looked at the paperwork and then came up with the correct name, and I was doing some ad-libbed stuff along the way. It just worked. It worked real well because when the camera was on Michael Keaton, I was in the background carrying on with another case so I just had to make up shit. Which is what I do. Don't get me bored, because I make up shit!

You've said that you don't want to play heavies anymore. If Tarantino asked you to play the heavy in one of his films, would you consider it?

Yes, I would, because if Quentin asked, I would probably do it because I know it would be something that had some substance to it. The thing is, it's not that I don't like doing heavies; I just don't like being stereotypical heavies. Just dumb guys waving guns around doing dumb shit. You don't have that in a Quentin Tarantino film. You don't do dumb shit. It's got purpose. It's got drive. It's got a whole subtext behind the character. Sure, I would do it. Hell yeah.

Tarantino said he took the role in Grindhouse because it reminded him of the kind of role you would have played. What are your thoughts on that?

I'd never heard that before. Well, that kind of takes me back. Geez. I don't know what to think about that. That's amazing. You just took me by surprise. I don't know. That's certainly gratifying to hear that he would say something like that, and I'm sure he meant it in a good way. I'm shocked. Color me shocked. That's a new color in the Crayon box. Shocked. Wow, that's cool. Things like that happen and they take you by surprise. Like when we were working on *Jackie Brown*, I really never got to work with Sam Jackson. He was in the courtroom, but we never really worked together. During a set up, we got to talk, the three of us. Samuel L. Jackson said, "One of my goals when I came to Hollywood was to make this happen for real and to do something with you." That just fills you up when somebody says something like that you don't know how to take it. It's a pretty big compliment. I really appreciate that. It's a nice sentiment. I think Quentin alluded to that on the special features *Jackie Brown* disc in a matter of fact. The meeting between Samuel L. Jackson and me. That was amazing.

Quentin's an amazing guy. He's very open, and very friendly. He's always been good to me. As a matter of fact, here's another thing that you get taken by surprise. The very first Scream Awards happened. He and Robert Rodriguez were getting an award for most inventive—they had strange categories for that thing. Quentin got up to accept his award and he said something to the effect of, "I take my hat off to any award show that recognizes the lifelong work of Sid Haig." Robert was pointing at me and bowing. Rob Zombie was sitting in front of me. He turned around and slapped me in the chest and said, "How's that for a fucking shout out?" I almost started to get a little teary. It was an amazing thing. Then, for the second Scream Awards, they worked it out so that I was presenting the award to him for Best Director. That was very cool. I asked the producers if I could deviate from the script just a little bit, taking no more than twenty seconds. So he came up to get his award and I hung on to it. I said, "I just want everyone to know that there was a point when my career was circling the drain, and this guy right here is the one who made me understand that this is where I have to be." I gave him his award. Then he—he had to top me, that fucker—said, "I was happy to do Hollywood that service." Okay, Quentin, you got me again, dammit. It's cool things like that that happen that—those are the kinds of things that keep you going when things get a little rough. When the work isn't there, but somebody says something like that. It has a tendency to keep you moving forward. Very supportive and encouraging guy. Quentin deserves everything he gets. Just a great guy.

CRAIG HAMANN

Craig Hamann conceived *My Best Friend's Birthday*, which he and Quentin Tarantino later co-wrote and co-directed on a meager budget of $5,000. In addition, the duo also co-wrote a treatment titled *The Criminal Mind* about a serial killer who baffles the police when he suddenly stops killing. Hamann has since done some screenwriting and has optioned *My Best Friend's Birthday*, which led to a falling out between he and Tarantino. Despite this, Hamann still praises Tarantino's vision and work.

In 1998, Hamann directed his first feature film, *Boogie Boy*, which he also wrote. The film was produced by *Pulp Fiction* co-writer Roger Avary and stars Marc Dacascos, Jaimz Woolvett, and Frederic Forrest.

I recall reading something about a "biological warfare" film that you and Quentin made in acting school. Could you tell me about that?

Warzone was shot on video by a bunch of us in 1982, and it eventually had nothing to do with any acting class, nor was it shot at an acting school. It involved three prisoners, played by Quentin, Rick Squeri, and myself, who are in a stockade at a secret U.S. Biological warfare facility. A biological war takes place, and the prisoners don't even know it. They manage to escape the stockade and go out and find some people who are still alive. Little by little, the prisoners figure out what's going on. They double-cross each other, etc. Finally, there's a violent showdown at the end.

This was written by Al Harrell, myself, and Todd Henschell. Al directed it. Todd and I produced it. QT was one of the stars.

It was a difficult shoot. Every location was stolen or shot at my house, and none of us knew what we were doing. But as with most no-budget film experiences, we all learned a lot.

You once called My Best Friend's Birthday *"fairly autobiographical." Could you elaborate on that a little bit?*

In *My Best Friend's Birthday*, the character Clarence was inadvertently getting Mickey into one mess after another. This is based loosely on QT's and my friendship. At that time, we were best friends. But Quentin could always find a way to mess things up for me. For example, Quentin had a habit of calling me late at night every time his car broke down, and no matter what kind of car he had, it *always* broke down. I'd have to go pick him up, and then he'd spend the night at my house. Well, I might have an acting audition or even a part on a TV show early the next morning, so I would need my sleep. But he'd call. I'd feel sorry for him and go pick him up. The next day I would be on the sound stage of some soap, where I was playing some role for a week, and I'd be half asleep. One time my car broke down on the way to pick him up after his car broke down. Things like that would always happen.

Another similarity we had to the characters, whether we knew it or not, was that Clarence and Mickey think they're the coolest guys going in their microcosmic world. Quentin and I had the same problem. We had all the answers, especially about what movies were good, bad, what actors were cool, and what actors had their heads up their butts.

Roger Avary, Quentin Tarantino, Rand Vossler, and yourself all worked on My Best Friend's Birthday. *Roger, Quentin, and yourself have all directed feature films now, and Rand co-produced* Natural Born Killers. *That's a hell of a crew for a film with a budget of $5,000.*

I think everyone but me knew they would be directing a film one day. Quentin certainly did. Roger had already finished some great Super-8 films. Rand was very technically well versed. I hadn't directed anything, and I was fairly technically illiterate. The tech side of things bores the shit out of me. QT was the same way. I don't think he was bored by the tech stuff, but he sure as hell was a lot more interested in the creative end. Of course, as you direct a film, you start to learn about the technical aspects.

It's been stated that Kevin Reynolds' Fandango *heavily influenced Quentin's contributions to* My Best Friend's Birthday. *Do you believe that's true, and if so, in what ways?*

Well, Fandango is just a good movie. If it had more influence on Quentin regarding *My Best Friend's Birthday* than, say, a good Howard Hawks movie, then I honestly don't know about it. The stylistic use of dialogue in some of Hawks' films influenced my writing in *My Best Friend's Birthday*, for example. Sure, Quentin and I talked about Fandango a lot because we both loved it. But you'd have to ask Quentin about it influencing his direction in *My Best Friend's Birthday*. He had a lot of influences, to be sure.

Looking back at My Best Friend's Birthday, *what is your assessment of the film today?*

Quentin once told me that *My Best Friend's Birthday* was his film school. I agree completely. The entire film was trial by fire. Long nights, no money, not much sleep, if any. But we learned a lot from just holding our noses and taking the plunge. In this way, *My Best Friend's Birthday* is a constant source of pride for me. I remember one asshole telling me that I'd never get the film done, and even if I did, it would be a piece of shit. I never told QT that the guy said this to me. Well, we did a good job, especially for two guys who didn't know what the hell we were doing. So, I think it was a good thing. And it was, without a doubt, all the better because Quentin and I did it together, always relying on our faith in one another throughout the entire ordeal. I'm not trying to leave out Rand, Roger, or anyone else, but the truth is, Quentin and I were the ones who decided to take on the task of making the movie.

I understand that you and Quentin worked on some other projects. Tell me about those.

Oh, maybe Quentin would give me some scenes written in pencil on notebook paper, and I would type it up for him. I'd correct grammatical mistakes and clean it up, but other than *My Best Friend's Birthday* and *The Criminal Mind*, I don't recall us working on any other project together. I did, however, type up his screenplays for him sometimes. Plus we used to sit together and cold read scenes from his screenplays; kind of act them out just to hear them.

One thing that I did do was help Quentin with his writing style. The first pages he gave to me to type up on *True Romance* are a good example. Back then it was called *The Open Road*. And in that screenplay, the lead character, Clarence, was writing a screenplay called *Natural Born Killers* as he was going through his own adventures.

Anyway, the first pages weren't that good. Not to say that QT's writing wasn't good, but he was hurting himself by overwriting. Hell, it took all day for him just to set up a scene. I told Quentin to trim everything. In fact, I said to Quentin, "With your writing, all anyone's going to care about is what are the characters doing, and what will they have to say about it?" Quentin came back a few days later with new pages that were very much like his lean and mean style we now see. Don't get me wrong. I did not create Quentin's style. I just helped him find it within his own work. It was already there. He deserves credit for the talent part, that's for sure.

You mentioned a treatment you and Quentin wrote called The Criminal Mind. *I understand that's a pretty solid concept as far as the story goes. As co-creator, have you ever considered doing anything with that?*

I have never considered doing anything with it, and I wouldn't do anything unless Quentin wanted to.

You did some overdubs on Reservoir Dogs. *Is that right?*

My voice is in several parts of Reservoir Dogs. Actually, I used to get paid to do voiceovers in films during the mid-eighties, especially bad films that were being doctored. Working with and for Quentin on the ADR sessions on *Reservoir Dogs* was a hoot. Roger was there, too. We all had fun.

You also served as an unofficial adviser of sorts on Pulp Fiction. *Tell me about that experience.*

I had a serious drug problem when I was younger. Because Quentin knew that, he asked me to meet with Uma Thurman and him one night at Toi's, which is a Thai restaurant. During our meeting, I discussed what it was like to overdose on heroin. I should know. I had done it. Uma did a good job in the film, and she used a lot of what I had told her. She's a talented actress, very smart, who picks things up quickly.

I also met with John Travolta and coached him about smack for his character. I like John. When I would go visit the *Pulp Fiction* set, I'd usually end up in John's trailer drinking iced tea with him. He's a major talent, in my view.

I agree.

By the way, I also gave Quentin some ideas regarding the Uma drug overdose scene in *Pulp Fiction*, which he used. I was flattered. However, some bozo wrote that I actually scripted and directed that scene. That's bullshit. I don't know where some of these idiots get these stupid ideas!

While we're discussing the drug scenes, as you mentioned, Quentin's Pulp Fiction, *as well as Roger Avary's* Killing Zoe, *and your own film,* Boogie Boy, *all deal with heroin use to some extent. Why do you think that is?*

I don't know why Quentin and Roger dealt with heroin use. I did it because I used to use the stuff, among a zillion other drugs, especially meth, and so I put that in my film. Since I was once a needle freak, I wrote about that as well. I've been clean for a long time now. In fact, I don't even drink alcohol now.

As a director in your own right, what do you think of Quentin's work, and what do you see as being his strongest asset?

    I believe Quentin is extremely creative and talented. The thing that I like about most of his work is that he has a signature of his own. You know, I can remember Quentin and I talking about Al Harrell, a friend of ours who is also a writer/director. We both determined that when Al writes or directs something, it doesn't really matter if it's good or bad, because Al will put his own unique take on it and make it interesting. I think Quentin is that way, too. I mean, a movie doesn't have to be good for me to like it. If the film was done by a director with vision, I can promise you that I'll find something to like about it, even if it's a fairly cheesy film.
    Quentin has his own vision. Like his films or not, they belong to him. And he really truthfully is someone who loves films. I hear people talk about how much they love film, and this includes a lot of so-called filmmakers, but when push comes to shove, their movies look like everyone else's movies. If they love film so much, why didn't they get something out of it that ends up belonging to just them? Quentin does that. When he watches a movie, he takes part of it home with him in his soul. I've always admired that about him, and I always will.

MONTE HELLMAN

Monte Hellman is best known to film aficionados as the helmer of such classic westerns as *The Shooting* and *Ride in the Whirlwind*, both of which starred a fresh-faced Jack Nicholson and Warren Oates. Hellman, an accomplished filmmaker, screenwriter, and producer, also directed the 1971 classic *Two-Lane Blacktop*. In 1991, Hellman met Quentin Tarantino, a would-be director who greatly admired his films, after reading his screenplay for *Reservoir Dogs*. After discussing cinema and becoming good friends, Hellman agreed to executive produce the young director's debut film.

At one point, you were interested in directing Reservoir Dogs *yourself. Is that right?*

Yes. I had been approached indirectly by [producer] Lawrence Bender through a friend of mine. They felt that having a director attached would make it easier to get the picture made. They set up a meeting between me and Quentin. I met with him, and just by coincidence, on the day we met, he had sold *True Romance*. He apologized for making me come to the meeting. He said that as much as he admired my work, he was now going to direct the movie himself. He could afford to do it now that he'd sold his screenplay. I told him I thought that was great, and that he would be the right director for it. He asked me if I would help him get it made, and that's what I did.

Just for fun, how might you have directed Reservoir Dogs *differently had you shot it?*

I think I probably would have done the whole thing differently, but that doesn't mean that I would have made a better film. I think he made the film as it should have been.

As a legendary filmmaker yourself, what do you see as being Tarantino's strengths?

He has tremendous strength as a writer, obviously. One of his greatest strengths as a director is his tremendous enthusiasm. He energizes everyone around him, because he is so in love with what he's doing, and the film. He somehow creates an excitement, just by *his* excitement.

I remember reading that you were adapting Elmore Leonard's novel Freaky Deaky, *with Tarantino producing. What is the current status of that project?*

I think it's kind of on a backburner. I don't know why. I think it's a project that Tarantino liked very much, but I think the other powers that be no longer share that enthusiasm. Perhaps because of the disappointing [box-office] results from *Jackie Brown*, they're less interested in Elmore Leonard.

Is that a project you still believe may one day come to fruition?

I wouldn't want to bet on it, either way. I really wouldn't know. I know that I've moved on to another project in particular, and other projects in general. I've kind of put that on the backburner myself.

At one time, Tarantino expressed an interest in writing a script for you to direct. He said it would be a remake of your film, Ride in the Whirlwind, *which would be relocated to the 1930s.*

That is something we did talk about, and he actually had it all worked out. He talked the whole script, actually. He had it all worked out in his head. He told me the whole story, and it would be terrific, but I don't know if or when he'll take the time to actually write it.

I remember that you and Tarantino were planning to executive produce a couple of films for one another. Is that something that's still going to happen?

No. That was a deal we had that we'd kind of worked out with a company. That's kind of gone by the wayside because of a conflict with his Miramax deal.

DENNIS HUMBERT

In the mid-1980s, Quentin Tarantino not only worked as a video clerk at Los Angeles' now-legendary Video Archives video store, but he damn near lived there. In addition to Tarantino, *Pulp Fiction* co-writer Roger Avary, author and former director of Rolling Thunder Films Gerald Martinez, and early-Tarantino collaborator Scott McGill also worked in the place. After Video Archives folded, co-owner Dennis Humbert (sixty-percent owner) tried his hand at screenwriting and also real estate.

Humbert sat down with me to reminisce on Tarantino and the gang's exploits at the legendary video store.

When did you first meet Quentin Tarantino?

Quentin was probably hired six or seven months after we opened. He was a customer. I never knew him until he was hired. I was still working as a manager at some casinos in Gardena in the daytime, and Quentin worked days, so our paths never crossed much initially. Quentin was a customer who worked at another video store in the area and he and co-owner Lance Lawson became friends.

Lance was amazed at this nineteen-year-old kid who had a photographic memory for movies and this general passion for movies. He offered him a job, and Quentin was delighted to accept it. His goal was always to be a movie director. Although he did take acting classes and so on and so forth, it was always his passion to be a director.

What kind of employee was Quentin?

Quentin was a pretty good employee. He always had a suggestion for somebody. When he spoke about film, he spoke knowledgeably. Quentin was a terrific salesman. I'm convinced that he sold his way into Hollywood. He used that salesmanship on a lot of our clients with movies. If Quentin liked a movie, he wouldn't let you go. He was like a dog hanging on to your pants, you know? He just wouldn't let you go until you'd rented that movie. Then when the customers would bring back the movie, they'd have debates and arguments about it. A lot of these were movies no one had ever heard of. When he was really sold on something, he had a genuine passion for it. He loved obscure movies. He loved "women in bondage" films and things like that. Of course his favorite movie was *Rio Bravo*, which happened to be one of mine, as well. One day we were discussing *The Man Who Shot Liberty Valance*, and we were talking about this one scene. And Quentin was mimicking Strother Martin, John Wayne, and Lee Marvin. He did the whole scene himself where Lee Marvin kicked over John Wayne's steak that James Stewart was carrying to him. He did the spiel, the whole scene verbatim. I said, "Quentin, did you just watch this movie yesterday or something?" I mean god, he had it down pat. He says, "No, my mom took me to see it when I was seven or eight." And he remembered all the dialogue verbatim!

And I thought, *geez, this guy's really got some kind of photographic memory*. There's something special about him. He just knew everything. I know when he came to work for us, he'd posed as a writer for some magazine and he'd interviewed twenty or so well-known directors in Hollywood. He got to be friends with one of them, who actually taught him a little bit about directing and shooting film. He was really creative. He would create sections on particular kinds of films in the store on his own. There would be something in the news that might apply, especially a death or someone winning an award. And he would know exactly what films to pull to make a special section for this event. He was quite remarkable.

There's a legendary story about Quentin attacking one of the customers. What do you know about that? Was he reprimanded for the incident?

I heard something about that. I'm not sure he physically attacked them. I really don't recall that. They probably kept that away from me. I've never seen him lose his temper. He's usually pretty mild and well mannered, very polite and courteous.

Describe the atmosphere at Video Archives.

You had four or five guys working a shift who were all good friends. When the store closed, they usually all went out to a movie together or went and hung out somewhere. They were all best friends who shared a love of movies. They got along really well. All of them dreamed of making it in the movie business. It was a pretty happy atmosphere.

Were you ever amazed by the number of Video Archives employees who went on to careers in the film industry?

Yeah. I just ran into Jerry Martinez at a wrestling event the other day. He told me he had a book published about blaxploitation films and that he was helping to run Rolling Thunder Films. I was kind of surprised to hear that. Of course Quentin started that company, Rolling Thunder Video, which was a name he got from us. We created a fictitious company called Rolling Thunder Video. There was this guy in a truck we'd buy X-rated tapes from and it would be all cash, so we created this invoice called Rolling Thunder Video so we could write it off. I guess Quentin took the title of that for his company.

Really?

I actually gave Quentin the whole premise for *True Romance*. He used to be fascinated by the poker casinos. I used to even take him down to the casinos and show him the surveillance system and how we used to catch card thieves. I used to tell him stories. There were some really interesting things that happened in those casinos. One day, I was telling Quentin about a guy I knew who bought a hooker for one of his new employees as a birthday present. This guy instructed the hooker not to tell the guy she was a hooker, and Quentin just thought that was a fascinating story. And that's how *True Romance* started out. He used that story I told him.

What are your most vivid memories of Quentin?

For Quentin, it wasn't at all unusual to watch five or six movies in a single night. He'd work until ten or eleven, and we had this thirty-five-inch Mitsubishi big screen TV, which was pretty rare at that time. We had that there in the store and Quentin would watch movies all night. We'd wake him up at nine or ten in the morning and he'd be asleep on the floor. He'd just get up and start working again. His enthusiasm for film is what I remember.

Several members of the old Video Archives crew found that Quentin often took real-life conversations and turned them into movie scenes. Are there any instances of this that you can remember?

There were several parts in *Reservoir Dogs* that he used from the stories I told him. He even used some of the names. I created the name Nice Guy Eddie for a guy named Eddie Carpinski who used to hang around the store. He was just a really nice guy. And being from the card clubs, we pretty much nicknamed everyone with some kind of name. In another scene in *Reservoir Dogs*, the characters discuss a girl who Superglued her husband's penis to his stomach. That's a true story that I told Quentin about and he used it. He used my best friend's name in the movie, Fred McGarr, and I guess the actor fucked it up and called him Frank McGarr. There were quite a few other lines in there that he used.

I was told that the "I'd fuck Elvis" line came from a conversation you had with Quentin once.

Quentin told me that seriously. He came up to me one day and he was serious. He looked at me dead seriously in the eye. We were watching *One Night with You*, and Quentin came up to me and said, "Dennis, I'm not a fag. But if I had to do it with any man, I'd do it with Elvis." [Laughs.] And I thought, *what a thing to say!* It was just so off the wall that it really cracked me up. But yeah, he really said that.

There is a story that Quentin purchased all of the videocassettes after Video Archives shut its doors. Is that true?

Yeah, he did. We were in big financial trouble. You know, Quentin probably paid us four or five times what those videos were worth. I was negotiating with his business manager, and Quentin and Lance was there, and they knew the values of used videos. His business manager had done his research and I said, "Let's have a little sidebar here." I took Lance out in the hall. I said, "Let's just ask Quentin for," I think it was $80,000. I said, "Let's just ask him if he'll give it to us for old time's sake." There were so many times I had fed Quentin and loaned him money and fixed his cars. I took care of Quentin. I was in a position to do that back then. So I went back into the meeting and said, "Quentin, will you give us $80,000 for these videos?" And his business manager said, "No, no, no, no!" And I just looked Quentin in the eye and he said, "Yeah, I'll give you $80,000."

It was nice. It was like payback time, you know? Because if I'd taken those movies to a dealership or something, I would have gotten like five or six thousand, tops. Five cents on the dollar or whatever. And you know, he didn't buy any of the X-rated films. Just all the rest. That was a really nice thing for him to do.

ANGELA JONES

Pennsylvania-bred actress Angela Jones began her career in the short 1991 Rob Braddock-directed *Curdled*. Quentin Tarantino then saw the film, liked both it and its lead actress, and cast her in *Pulp Fiction* as Esmerelda Villa Lobos ("Esmerelda of the Wolves"). He then cast her in a feature-length remake of *Curdled*, which he executive produced. Other films on Angela Jones' filmography include *Underworld, Children of the Corn V: Fields of Terror,* and *Man on the Moon*. She also appeared in the Tarantino-directed episode of *E.R.*, "Mother's Day."

The beautiful Jones found time in her busy schedule to sit down with me and talk about all things Quentin Tarantino.

I understand that Quentin Tarantino cast you for Pulp Fiction *after seeing you in the short version of* Curdled. *Is that right?*

Yeah. *Curdled* was originally a short film I did in graduate school, and they showed it at a film festival in Italy while I was still in school. Our producer was there with it, and he said he met this guy named Quentin Tarantino who had this movie called *Reservoir Dogs*. He watched the short and he really loved it. He wanted to meet me. I was still in graduate school in Florida at the time. Then, when I moved to Los Angeles, it was right when *Reservoir Dogs* opened here. We met at a restaurant on Sunset Boulevard, and he was just great. From the moment I met him, he was incredibly supportive of my work.

He told me a little bit about *Pulp Fiction* and that he was thinking of putting a character who was similar to Gabriella in there, but he wasn't sure yet. He was still in the process of writing the script. But he really loved the character I played, Gabriella, and we talked about that. He was like a friend right from the start.

What was your reaction the first time you read the screenplay for Pulp Fiction?

The first time I saw it, he had come to a play I was performing in. He was carrying around this huge notebook with all the scenes written out by hand. I could barely read it. [Laughs.]

Quentin does have rather distinct handwriting.

Yes, he does. You've seen his handwriting?

In fact-checking for this book, he wrote out some stuff by hand.

Anyway, the script was great, but I had to read it again, you know? On paper, it was like nothing I had ever read before. A lot of scripts use a format and they all seem very similar, but this one jumped back and forth in time and all the characters spoke like real people. That's extremely rare. He tried to make it as believable as possible. Quentin's characters really talked. Most of the time they don't do that. I mean they do, but these characters spent time beyond. . . .

They were very real people.

Yeah! Yeah, so I loved it.

At the time you were working on Pulp Fiction, *did you have any idea just how big this film was going to be?*

I had no idea at all. No idea. I'm from Pennsylvania, and I remember telling my mother about *Reservoir Dogs*, which was his first film, and it had never even played there. I'm from Pittsburgh, but from a really small town just outside there. So if you wanted to see an independent film there, you had to travel into the city. So my mother asked if she was going to see the movie, and I told her she'd probably have to travel to the city because it probably wouldn't play on that many screens. And I had no idea it was going to be as big as it was. Not at all. I didn't even know if my part was gonna stay in the movie, you know? The movie came in at two-and-a-half hours, and I really thought my part would be the first one to go. Quentin said, "No, no, no. It's in there." So no, I had no idea.

The scene between Butch and Esmerelda was cut a little bit in the theatrical release. Which version of the scene do you prefer?

That's a good question. I guess I prefer the longer one because I remember when we shot it, he wanted it to look like film noir, just taking a lot of time in between the words. He just really set the pace for that. So when I had to go in and do some of the ADR work—the voiceover stuff—he told me they'd cut out the air between the lines. But then they ended up putting them back in for the director's cut. I kind of like the longer one because we spend more time with each other, just getting to know one another. I think the scene stands apart from the movie like a little movie in itself. It almost doesn't fit, but they just spent more time together getting to know each other. She's really into his story, you know.

Although it does slow down the pace of the film, I think the longer version is much more realistic. Instead of just jumping into the conversation about, "You just killed this guy," it's more drawn out the way a conversation like that would actually be.

Yeah, it's like, *is he gonna kill me or is he not gonna kill me?* But I really want to know, one way or the other. So yeah, it is more natural.

What is your reaction to Pulp Fiction's *being named to the American Film Institute's Top 100 Films list?*

I think it's very cool. I think it's a great film. It really stands out. These people. Maybe the plot is not so much like the first act, second act, third act, but these people spend time talking and getting to know each other. They're bad guys and criminals, but they're likable.

You also appear in Underworld, *which is another film I really like. It seemed very much inspired by the work of Tarantino. Was that one of the reasons you chose the project?*

When I read the script, it was mainly the two guys. So much of the script was just the two guys talking, Denis Leary and Joe Mantegna. Then, when I went in for the audition, they were like, "Just pick any girl," but all the female roles were very similar. So I knew when I met the director that this was a great project—for male actors. [Laughs.] But I like the feel of it.

Quentin executive produced the feature-length version of Curdled. *To what extent was he involved with the project?*

He was involved from the very start. He used the same writer, director, producer from the original film, and we were all friends from school. I guess they were sending him scripts back and forth from Florida. What was definitely great was that he told them they had to use me. [Laughs.] He had an influence, but he didn't overshadow the project like, "You have to make it this way" or "You have to make it that way." Basically, he just let us make the movie we wanted to make, which I think is great. At that time, he was shooting *From Dusk Till Dawn*. He was really supportive of all of us and the different ideas they had. But I think they were pretty collaborative on that.

Was Quentin responsible for your appearing in "Mother's Day," the episode he directed of E.R., *or was this just a coincidence?*

Well, I got called in on the audition. I'm sure he had something to do with that. But I did have to audition, and he was there for that. I'm sure he had some influence on it, but I did have to read for it. It was great to work with him again. It was fun—a lot of fun.

LINDA KAYE

Linda Kaye is a longtime friend of Quentin Tarantino and has appeared in brief roles in both *Reservoir Dogs* and *Pulp Fiction*. Although she was not employed at Video Archives, she was considered "one of the group," which consisted of future filmmakers Quentin Tarantino and Roger Avary, as well as Russell and Rand Vossler, Gerald "Jerry" Martinez, Stevo Polyi, Rowland Wafford, and another non-employee, Steve Martinez. Kaye also edited and sometimes typed Tarantino's early screenplays. She also appeared in *My Best Friend's Birthday*, an early film directed by Tarantino and Craig Hamann. In 1990, Tarantino and Rand Vossler approached Kaye's parents, Chuck and Gloria Walker, for money to fund *Natural Born Killers*. Although the Walkers were intrigued by what they heard of the project and were supportive of Tarantino, they were unable to give the would-be filmmakers the money they needed due to financial difficulties.

Linda Kaye has also worked as a stuntwoman in what she calls "a lot of bad horror movies." Her stuntwoman credits include *Shocker*, *Return of the Swamp Thing*, *The Seventh Sign*, and *Bad Dreams*.

Tell me a little bit about your friendship with Quentin Tarantino, and how you first met him.

The first time I met him was at Video Archives. This had to be, I don't know, mid-1980s. I went in there and it was mid-afternoon, and the place was dead. There was no one there, and they had a big-screen television, which was a big, new thing at the time, blasting some movie. I don't know what it was; I think it might have been *The Godfather*. I was over there looking at movies, and Quentin came over and said very congenially, "Hi, can I help you?" And I told him there was this one actor I really liked, and I didn't know what other movies he'd been in. And he said, "What actor? Maybe I know." And I said, "I doubt it. He's really an obscure guy. He was in this movie called *Body Heat*." And he's like, "Oh, sure, *Body Heat*." And I was like, yeah, thinking to myself, sure, this guy knows. I mean, *Body Heat* made no money. I loved it, but I figured no one else had seen it. He's like, "Who? William Hurt?" I told him no and then he says, "Well, it must be Mickey Rourke." He's like, "Oh, sure, the arsonist." Wow. Yeah, that's right. Now all my attention is focused on this big goofy guy who's just sitting there, just grinning and nodding. And he says, "Well, let's see. There are rumors that he's going to be in this movie with Kim Basinger about some sex thing." Of course he was talking about *9 ½ Weeks*. And this was before that movie was ever even made. He went on to tell me some other things Mickey Rourke had done, which was just little crap I'd never heard of. I was just so impressed with this guy's knowledge of film. And he was like, "Oh, did you know that *Body Heat* was written by Lawrence Kasdan?" Then he went on to give me Lawrence Kasdan's biography. Then he went on to tell me about *Silverado*, which Kasdan had written and was just about to be filmed.

Quentin just knew so much. I asked him how he knew about all this stuff, and he said, "Well, I watch movies all day and I am really interested in it. I want to be a director someday." And I said, "You know what? I can just see that." I kind of closed my eyes and gestured my hands out, kind of like a spread, you know, like opening an imaginary banner. And I said, "I can see it now—a film by Quentin Tarantino." I said, "That just sounds like a director's name." I looked him in the eyes and said, "I just know you're going to make it one day." And he thanked me. From the moment I met him, I believed in him. And when he finally did make it, I pulled him aside and said, "Remember, Quentin? Remember that day at Video Archives, the first day I met you?" And he's like, "Yeah, I remember." I knew it. I just knew it.

And it was a really nice feeling, in my lifetime, to see him have success. And I don't think I've said that about anyone else, although I've believed it about Jerry [Martinez] and Russell [Vossler], because they're so talented at what they do. And Quentin, I could just tell had a vision. A sort of, I don't know, just that type of personality. All that knowledge. He just had to make it. I knew it. I didn't think he'd make it overnight and scream wildly to the top of the ladder like he did. And frankly, I'm not sure that's something I would wish on someone. But it did happen, and I think our friendship grew from that point.

We had a mutual interest in film, and he told me it was rare to find a "chick" who liked Mickey Rourke because Mickey Rourke was sort of this bad boy. Quentin found quickly that I wasn't the typical chick in a lot of ways. He and I went to a few movies together and stayed up until all hours of the night talking. Our friendship grew pretty quickly, but steadily. Then I got introduced and exposed to the rest of the group, which would have been other employees at Video Archives at the time that seemed to hang out together. That was actually a pretty hip place to work at the time. It was a fun place to work. I used to go and just hang out for hours. I was not getting paid, but I would help them put away videos and do stuff, you know, just to kind of be doing something. And that went on for five or six years—at least until the early '90s. And then, unfortunately, things started happening and the group started to dispel. Then Quentin made it, and everyone was happy about that. I remember they had some Quentin things up in the video store for a while.

What are your most vivid memories of Quentin Tarantino?

A couple of times he asked me to proofread his screenplays. He gave me the typed or printed off copies, and I sat reading and going over every page with him, giving him feedback; mostly compliments. And the little stuff I did have to correct was very minor, nothing crucial. Nothing content-wise. There was a scene in [the first draft of] *Natural Born Killers* where this guy came into a diner with a Bible and he was screaming at the top of his lungs and ripping pages out of this Bible, throwing them in the air. And these pages were fluttering down. The guy was just a fanatic. I told Quentin how much I loved that scene, and he just gave me that laugh of his and said, "I met a guy like that once." I said, "Quentin, it scares me the kind of people you've met." And I just told him the scene was wonderful because the way he wrote it just made the character seem like such a fanatic, ripping the pages from the Bible, so frenzied and foamy-mouthed over whatever it was he was preaching. I thought that was great.

We all, as a group, used to go out pretty regularly. We would all go down to Westwood as a group. You know, one or two carloads of us; maybe six or eight of us. And that would be Stevo [Polyi], Quentin, me, Russell; Not Rand [Vossler] so much. Rand came into the picture later on. Anyway, Roger [Avary], Rowland [Wafford], and then the occasional girlfriend. We all would go to see whatever movie had just come out and was hot that Friday night. Quentin was just so much fun to take with us. He was just so entertaining. We'd all be standing in line at the theater, just kind of looking at our money, standing in line, and he'd say, "Hey you guys, wouldn't it be cool if, all of sudden, right now, somebody just, like, walked right up to us . . . and killed us? Just, like, blasted us with machine guns. Wouldn't that be cool?" And we all just kind of looked at each other like, *Yeah, that'd be cool.* And he was like, "Just think. Wouldn't that be weird? Just so random, you know?" And we were all trying to understand how a thing like that could be cool. I think his definition of cool meant, you know, if it were a scene in a movie—not if it really happened. I said, "God, Quentin. If that really happened then we'd all be dead and that would be really sad." And he'd still be like, "Yeah, but it'd be cool." He defended it. He completely defended it. He'd say little random things like that that would just make us all look at each other. It was then that we knew why we took him with us. Where else are you gonna get entertainment like that? Certainly not in the theater. And that was just one of a jillion things he would say.

His arguments about film have been well documented. Have you ever been involved in, or witnessed, such an argument with him?

I don't remember a lot of them because I, as a peace lover, sort of tended to pair off with Russell. Russell and I would just sort of whisper to each other, "Isn't this silly how they're carrying on?" Whenever any of that would happen, I tried not to ever argue about films—especially not with someone as knowledgeable as Quentin.

Do any of their arguments stand out in your mind?

None of them specifically stand out. All I really know is that there were some films that Quentin thought were overrated and some he thought were terribly underrated. He used to love sort of cheap, B-movie type things. Exploitation films. Ones that you normally would call cheesy, he revered. He told us all who Jackie Chan was before any of us ever knew. He just had a memory that was amazing. He could watch the credits and practically tell you who the wardrobe mistress' second assistant was on some obscure little 1982 indie film. It was just astounding. Sometimes, just for amusement we would ask him weird stuff like who stunt coordinated a certain movie. And he'd know. He'd always know. It was like the Mickey Rourke thing all over again.

Many of his friends have made statements that later appeared as dialogue in his films. Are you aware of any real-life incidents or conversations that have made their way into his work?

Yeah, I am. There was one, although I'm not sure it ever made it into the actual film. But he did it. He even told me what it was. I commented to him that "this sounds familiar," and he said, "Well, it should. You said it."
The man's line was, "I guess I'm just stupid." I think prior to this the man had said something like, "I didn't think you liked me" or "I didn't know you cared" or something. Then he said, "I guess I'm just stupid." Then she said, "You're not stupid, you're just wrong." That's what I had said to him one day, and he ended up writing it into something. I said, "Did I say that?" He said "yeah," and I said, "It sounds so much like a movie line now, but at the time it just seemed like the truth." And he said something

to the effect of, "Well, maybe that's why it sounds so good as a movie line."

That's interesting. I wasn't aware that was something that happened to anyone else other than me. Shame on me for being self-centered, I guess. I wasn't aware there were actually other things lifted like that.

Do you have any knowledge of his earlier projects, and if so, what do you remember about them?

Yeah, *My Best Friend's Birthday*. Quentin asked me one night to be in it. All I had to do was sit on this guy's lap. This was in the mid-eighties, around '86 or '87. He asked me to be in it. The scene took half the night. Rand was the cameraman and/or director of photography. It was in somebody's apartment over in a very scary part of town. Sort of Imperial Highway near Aviation, or Inglewood. That was the neighborhood. I think it might have been one of Quentin's old apartments when he lived in sort of a badass black neighborhood, for lack of a better term. This scene was supposed to take an hour, and it took about seven. And I remember I was late going over to my boyfriend's that night, and he got so mad at me that we had this huge fight that ended up leading to our breaking up. And I came back to Quentin's all upset. Quentin was involved in the film and all of its little problems. We had lighting problems and the neighbors kept banging on the ceiling saying, "Shut the fuck up!" I mean, this was at two in the morning and we were still at it, saying the same lines over and over. That had to get old for neighbors after awhile.

I asked for a copy of *My Best Friend's Birthday*. I was shown a videotape copy of it. It was scratchy. It was hard to hear. Since I was there for the filming, I was able to laugh and enjoy it. But somebody seeing it for the first time wouldn't have understood a thing. It didn't seem wonderful at all. I felt bad that Quentin was using it as a sort of calling card because I thought, Jesus, if you weren't there for the filming, you just wouldn't get the film.

I remember one thing Quentin came up with that I thought was just brilliant, and I don't remember hearing this anywhere else. Quentin and I were talking about a scene for some early film that he wanted to do and didn't have the budget for. He said, "There's a girl on a bed talking to a guy and she needs to brutally murder him. Hack him to pieces." And he goes, "I just don't have the budget for those kind of effects." Then he said, "So here's my plan." He proceeded to tell me. I believe there was some music playing in the background like, you know how an old-fashioned record player gets to the end of the record and goes *Kachunk! Kachunk! Kachunk!* Then the needle lifts up, goes back to the beginning of the record and sits down and plays the record again, right? Well, at the end of the music, there was that silence when the needle went to the end of the record. During that time, you could hear dialogue. The conversation was becoming heated, and their voices were escalating. Then you see the needle go to the beginning of the record. And then he said he would slowly pan around the room, doing a complete 360, starting at the bed and going around the room, around, around, around, just showing all the little crap on the wall—the little trinkets on the dusty shelves, the moonlight streaming through the slits in the blinds. The music is still going, so you can't hear anything. When the camera comes all the way around again, you see her sitting on the bed, bathed in blood.

I said, "Quentin, that's brilliant. That's fantastic. That way you avoid having to show the thing. Oh, my God. It's inspired. It's Hitchcockian." I was just going on and on because I thought so much of it. And it's funny how a low budget will force you into creative solutions that actually, even with a huge budget, you'd be wise to go with anyway. I don't think I need to keep selling it. It speaks for itself. You don't need to see somebody getting hacked to pieces, but you can see the aftermath. And you can't hear it because of this record playing. Everything is implied. Then, the next time you see it, and you're seeing this 360, you know what's happening. You know this guy's being hacked to pieces.

Are there any elements of Quentin's personal life that you see reflected in his work?

He seems to like feet. Um, let me be delicate. I didn't get to see the whole screenplay of *Pulp Fiction*. I was just given the pages that I had to do with and that was it. When I finally saw the movie, I had to laugh because they were going on about this whole foot massage thing. And I'll admit it: Quentin's given me a few foot massages, but I think he's probably given them to lots of girls. It was really just a thing between friends. It wasn't. . . . I don't mean to quote *Pulp Fiction*, but it didn't mean anything the way he made it sound in the movie. We were such good friends at that point that, you know, if Quentin had a sister he would have rubbed her feet, too. And I'm not implying any incest, okay? Although I can't see him doing it for a guy friend, it seemed not inappropriate at the time.

Quentin also had a thing for Barbie dolls. Not a weird thing. Nothing bizarre or unnatural, but he did collect them.

I've heard he collects quite a few things. Mostly movie memorabilia.

Not to say that he didn't, but all I really remember him collecting was these Barbie dolls. One time, I remember, we were all at Quentin's Hollywood apartment, and I remember we were all teasing Quentin about these Barbie dolls he had. I think it was Rand, or possibly Stevo, who implied some unnatural attraction to them. He said something like, "Uh, Quentin, is there anything that you'd like to tell us about these Barbie dolls and you?" And he'd usually just say something like, "Shut up," you know?

Other than the feet, which was always a good thing, I think I probably miss that most about our friendship. As much as I miss chatting with him about the good old days or movie trivia, God, I miss those foot rubs! [Laughs.]

How did you become involved with Reservoir Dogs *and* Pulp Fiction?

I got a phone call from Russell, and he told me there was a phone call that had come in from Quentin saying he wanted me to play a small part in his movie. "What movie?" This was the first I'd heard of it, and Russell said, "Well, it looks like Quentin's got a director's deal and he's filming a movie." And I said,

"Great." So I called and they said, "Can you come in on this date?" They were like, "This is what we want you to do."

I don't think Quentin knew that I had been in the hospital. I'd just gotten over a bout with a pretty serious disease. I had a spinal injury-slash-illness, which resulted in paralysis. I was in the hospital about eleven months and in a wheelchair for about another year after that. And this actually forced me to retire as a stuntwoman, where I'd had some success. It was a good thing I was a stuntwoman, because they said had I not been in such outstanding physical shape I probably never would have walked again.

So Russell told me about *Reservoir Dogs*. I did it. I went. And when I got there, I was kind of expecting Quentin to be the same old Quentin. It had only been a year and a half since I'd talked to him. And it didn't seem that long, but I was cautioned by somebody—maybe Rand—that Quentin "wasn't quite himself." I was told that he was "very into this directing thing, so don't be surprised if he isn't normal." Something like that. And things really weren't normal. I guess I expected him to throw his arms around me and say, "Hi!" Instead, he just looked at me, nodded and said, "They'll fit you for wardrobe now." He did make a point of sitting next to me at lunch that day. I was feeling very poorly and had gained a lot of weight, having been in the hospital for so long, and I was walking very stiffly, like Frankenstein. I hadn't quite gotten my sea legs back, as it were, from being sick.

I was very thankful for the work, and I told him, and he let me go and see the dailies, which were great. I was pulled out of a car and thrown on the ground by Steve Buscemi, who was just wonderful to work with. He was really a character. It was the first time I'd met [producer] Lawrence Bender, too. He seemed very nice. He played a cop who got shot. And he was producing. I'd never heard of him before this. He reminded me a little of Jeremy Irons, facially, and I've always liked Jeremy Irons, so I took an immediate liking to Lawrence Bender.

Then, the same thing happened with *Pulp Fiction*. I was at the hospital and my beeper went off. This time I was at the hospital for a different reason. I think one of my family members was ill. Anyway, I got a beep. It was Russell, telling me that Quentin's company had called again and they wanted me back for another movie. I went, "Wow. Cool." So I went and did *Pulp Fiction*.

This time Quentin was saying that he was everywhere. He was being interviewed. *Reservoir Dogs* was very big within the industry, and he was getting a lot of attention. Meanwhile, I see this cast of dozens of famous people. I'm looking at Bruce Willis and John Travolta, and saying to myself, "God!" I had heard all these actors were working for scale, and I was a little stunned. I guess word of *Reservoir Dogs* had spread and it had made a little name for itself, so all these actors wanted to do *Pulp Fiction* and were willing to work for nothing. So I was pleased and delighted to be working on the film.

ROBERT KURTZMAN

Robert Kurtzman is probably best known for his special effects makeup as the "K" in the now-legendary KNB Efx team. He also directed the cult favorite *Wishmaster*. Sadly, although he received a story credit for his work on *From Dusk Till Dawn*, many fans still have no idea the film wasn't actually conceived by Quentin Tarantino. Before Tarantino entered the picture, *From Dusk Till Dawn* was just an idea floating around in the special effects wizard's head. Then it took shape in the form of a twenty-page treatment penned by Kurtzman. He then enlisted Tarantino to write the screenplay, which he intended for his own directorial debut. Things didn't quite work out the way Kurtzman envisioned them, and the rest is history. While with KNB Efx, Kurtzman worked on the special effects makeup for *Reservoir Dogs*, *Pulp Fiction*, *From Dusk Till Dawn*, and both *From Dusk Till Dawn* sequels.

Because Kurtzman is a fan of Tarantino's work and remains a proud father figure in regards to *From Dusk Till Dawn*, he happily agreed to be interviewed for this book.

How did you come up with the concept for From Dusk Till Dawn?

My inspiration for *Dusk* came from my love of low-budget features like *Assault on Precinct 13* and *Race with the Devil*. *Dusk* was always intended to be a drive-in movie. In fact, when I was younger I spent almost every weekend at the drive-in. They would run all night "from dusk till dawn" horror films like *Night of the Living Dead*, *Zombie*, *Dawn of the Dead*, etc. I wanted to make a gritty, contained vampire tale—isolate the characters in a setting like *Assault* and do battle with the undead. I conceived *Dusk* as a low-budget indie film, which later ballooned into something much bigger.

How did you hook up with Quentin Tarantino?

My partner on Dusk, John Esposito, was originally going to write the screenplay based on my treatment. But he had to leave for six months to go to Maine, where they were shooting his film, *Stephen King's Graveyard Shift*. So we both decided to look for another writer to do the first draft. We started getting script samples from writers, and through Scott Spiegel and David Goodman, both Sam Raimi alumni, we heard about Quentin. We called him up and he sent over several scripts he'd already completed. The scripts were *Natural Born Killers, True Romance,* and *Reservoir Dogs*. Well, obviously, we had never read anything quite like them before. What balls! What dialogue! He was perfect for our tale of criminals on the lam who walk right into the den of Hell! Shortly after receiving the scripts, we hooked up together and soon found we were into the same movies—John Woo, Jackie Chan, Lucio Fulci, etc. Quentin told me we were the first people who ever hired him to write anything. It wasn't much. Only fifteen hundred dollars. But, at that point in both of our careers, it was a lot of money. This was around 1990 or so.

You originally intended for From Dusk Till Dawn *to be your own directorial debut. Obviously things didn't work out that way. What happened?*

Yes, *Dusk* was conceived to be my directorial debut. From 1990 to 1995, we shopped the script around town. People just thought the script was too hardcore. Lots of people passed on it even after *Reservoir Dogs* came out and was an indie hit. Then *Pulp Fiction* came out, and suddenly things started to change. The same people who told us the script was shit were now telling us it was a masterpiece. Standard Hollywood bullshit, right? Well, after several deals that almost happened and had us pulling out our hair over negotiations that went south, we finally made a deal with producers Mier Teper and Gianni Nunnari. Then Robert Rodriguez became interested in the project after Quentin showed him a copy of the script. At this point, we knew the project was going to become much bigger than we'd ever intended. Robert was hot, and we were just exhausted after five years of beating the pavement. We wanted to see this picture get made. So I stepped aside as director.

Had you directed the film when you wanted to, what differences would we see between your version and the film Robert Rodriguez made?

It would have been a much smaller picture. Several million dollars. Not the seventeen million dollars it ended up at. A lot of the effects work was true to what I had envisioned. In fact, a lot of the design work I'd done for the film was kind of rolled over when Robert came aboard. Robert had never handled an effects picture like this before, so he trusted me and KNB to work out a lot of stuff. Myself and storyboard artist John Bisson spent a lot of time with Robert working out all the action effects sequences. Robert brought the whole Aztec theme to the picture—the look of The Titty Twister, which I thought was great. Robert is also an incredible editor, and that brought a whole different kind of energy to the picture.

How much different was Quentin's initial draft of the script from your original treatment?

The biggest difference would be that the hotel was never in the treatment. After the Geckos rip off Benny's World of Liquor, they encounter the family on the road after their car breaks down. Then it's off to the border. After that, it's pretty faithful to the treatment. Everything at The Titty Twister is faithful.

I understand that the Ezekiel 25:17 monologue that Samuel L. Jackson uses in Pulp Fiction *originally appeared in Quentin's first draft of* From Dusk Till Dawn.

Yes, Ezekiel was in the early draft, but Quentin called me and asked if he could use it in his new script, *Pulp Fiction*. I had no problem as long as he wrote something new for *Dusk*.

Did you ever consider directing one of the From Dusk Till Dawn *sequels?*

Wishmaster came along about the time they were looking for directors on the *Dusk* sequels, and I was more interested in doing something original that didn't have a two or a three after its title. Plus, *Wishmaster* was going theatrical and the *Dusk* sequels were going straight to tape.

KNB Efx has worked on some of Quentin's other films, as well. Could you tell me a little bit about that?

On *Reservoir Dogs*, we did all the blood stuff and the ear gag. On *Pulp Fiction*, we did the guy's head exploding in the car and the body of his that they carry out, as well as some of the gruesome stuff in the basement bondage scene that got cut out for gore. Bruce Willis splits the guy with the sword. Uma's needle impalement. Other than Dusk, most of Quentin's films are not very effects heavy.

As a filmmaker yourself, what do you see as being Quentin's strengths?

Quentin is a master with dialogue, and he has no fear when approaching his characters. He's got a great sense of style. Especially in his selection of music in his films. The soundtracks are great.

STEVE MARTINEZ

Artist Steve Martinez was one of the few video store employees to be accepted into Quentin Tarantino and Roger Avary's Video Archives group in the 1980s. Steve's brother, Gerald, worked in the store and has remained one of Tarantino's closest associates. (Gerald Martinez was the head of Tarantino's now-defunct Rolling Thunder Pictures imprint, as well as the co-author of *What It Is, What It Was.*) When Tarantino was filming *Pulp Fiction,* he commissioned his old pal Steve Martinez to paint a portrait of Uma's Thurman's Mia Wallace, which appears in the film.

Could you tell me a little bit about the first time you met Quentin Tarantino?

It was 1984. My brother Jerry was working with Quentin. I remember that Quentin would come over to the house. He'd always pick up Jerry and they'd watch a movie. But he would never come in. He'd always be outside with the car running and Jerry would run outside to meet him, so he was sort of a shadowy figure. This was in 1983, maybe '84, and I finally met him. I'd go into the video store to see Jerry, and then I got to know Quentin. I saw right away he had a great sense of humor. He was a very funny guy, and I tried to impress my own humor upon, to see what he thought of it. I guess he liked it, because we became friends, too. I never worked at the video store, but we saw plenty of each other.

Are there any specific memories of Quentin that really stand out in your mind?

The scene from *Reservoir Dogs*, where they're talking and they're all arguing about the tip. You know that one? Maybe you already know this. Steve Buscemi is Mr. Pink and he's the one guy who doesn't want to leave a tip. Of course, Quentin plays one of the other guys trying to get him to tip the waitress and so on. Well, that was actually a case of art imitating life from when we would all go to Denny's or wherever. And Quentin was Mr. Pink—he wouldn't tip.

So that was taken from real life. Then we'd all get into a big fight because he wouldn't tip. The arguments the character is giving are the real-life arguments we heard from Quentin. We'd all go out to have dinner together, and we all knew, *Okay, we're gonna have to put up with this after the meal when it comes time to pay.* I thought that was pretty funny because the roles are reversed in the film.

Quentin was very enthusiastic, and I believe that's part of his success. I think that if you spent time with him, even way back then, you'd walk away with a real high because he was very positive. He really lifts you up, and I think he brings that to his films. I think when he works with people, he tries to create a really positive atmosphere. He was just a really enthusiastic guy. Sometimes he would drive me a little bit nuts, though, because it was always just the one subject—movies. I used to give him a hard time about that.

There are so many stories about Quentin's exploits that it's become difficult to discern what is real and what is legend. Have you seen anything about him in print that you know wasn't true? One story that's been going around for quite some time is that he beat up a customer at Video Archives. Do you know that story? Is that true?

[Laughs.] Yeah, it's true. I wasn't there to see it, but it happened. The guy was a pretty little guy, I think. I was a little bit unhappy with Quentin for deciding to pummel him because he was maybe a bit of a jerk, but. . . . It's a little bit like his later shenanigans. He was getting into trouble there for a time. He likes to maybe be a little bit of a tough guy. I think he took that opportunity on a lesser opponent—unduly, I think—and battered him. But I wasn't there for it, and for what it's worth, I heard afterwards that Quentin felt really badly about it. I think it was as he was beating him, he was sort of like, "Why did you make me do this?" But I'm sure the guy, to some degree, had it coming. But yeah, it's a true story. Quentin went over the counter and tackled him. He was whaling away on him. One time I arrived at the store, and I went out to Quentin's car and took out his jacket. I was going to wear it as sort of a joke, but he came out of the store right at that moment. He didn't know it was me and he was ready to rumble. So yeah, that's a true story.

As far as reading anything I knew to be untrue, I'm sure I have. I just don't remember it right off. I know often times they get the location of Video Archives wrong. In one book, I talked to the guy writing it, and when the book came out, I was mentioned as "Chris" Martinez.

Quentin's love for movies has been well documented. Do you have any specific memories relating to that?

I remember once we were all hanging out over at Jerry's apartment and Quentin was taking a nap. Then he woke up, and this was like nine or so. The first words out of Quentin's mouth were, "Let's go see a movie." I thought that was pretty funny. And again, I would always give him a hard time about that, but he was single-minded and he knew what he wanted to do.

It was pretty much non-stop, to the point of obsession. He wasn't afraid to let anyone know what he knew. He got us all interested in Sonny Chiba, and we would all get together on the weekend to watch *Shadow Warriors*. He was usually the first one to know about these things, and quite often, his tastes were correct. So we became Sonny Chiba fans, and we'd meet every weekend and we'd trade places. Everybody would take a turn hosting it on Sunday night. That was in 1989. Again, that was his idea. And you know, he really loved those blaxploitation movies.

I know that Quentin got into a number of disagreements with the other guys over films. Do you remember any of those arguments?

He had some funny arguments. He would stick to his guns, but I think when you're wrong, you're wrong. And I don't know if he was just being contrary or just trying to be overly cool by being so outrageous. But he would have these opinions like *Psycho II* was better than the original *Psycho*. He thought *Rocky II* was superior to the first *Rocky*. Really outrageous. Especially the *Psycho* argument. *Psycho* is considered a classic. I'm not a movie guy, but I think that's the general consensus. But if you listened to him long enough, he would almost start to make sense. He had some wild opinions. [Laughs.] I almost doubt he really believed some of them. He may have been just saying that to be saying it. He was very staunch in his opinions.

Jerry came in there and he was a big Alfred Hitchcock fan. And I think Quentin got him and exposed him to other things—stuff like the French new wave. Quentin was a huge Brian De Palma fan. There was one De Palma movie he just loved. Jeez, which one was it?

Blow Out?

Oh, he loved *Blow Out!* But that's not the one I'm trying to think of. Oh, yeah, it was *Body Double*. He loved *Body Double*. He would say these things were superior to Hitchcock's films. Even though they were sort of homages or remakes of Hitchcock, they were nonetheless superior. Things like that would sort of rankle our nerves.

There's another thing I remember about Quentin. He was a very good listener. He just is. That's something he has. I don't think I'm a great listener, but like a lot of people, I just sort of wait my turn. He really listens and, as well known, kind of soaks up information so he can use it again.

Do you remember any other specific statements or incidents from real life that turned up in one of his screenplays or films? I've heard that the "I'd fuck Elvis" line from True Romance *came from a conversation between Quentin and [Video Archives manager] Dennis Humbert.*

I think he may have said that. I don't know about that one

specifically. Actually I don't think that line was all that original. I heard it, but I think Burt Reynolds said something to that effect, only about Errol Flynn, in a movie once. So I don't know that that line was really that original.

I know as far as the scenario goes in *True Romance*, Christian Slater sitting there and a girl comes in and sits right next to you and you're watching a Kung Fu movie—that was Quentin's fantasy. At the time I knew that. Then afterwards, you go out and have pie and talk about the movie. That was Quentin's dream date. He expressed that to me. We talked about girls on occasion. You know, we talked about all kinds of things. That's just his dream—his idea date.

Have you ever seen any other elements of his personal life reflected in his work? Linda Kaye told me Quentin likes feet.

Oh, right. Good point. He does love feet. He has a foot fetish. That's a definite sexual turn-on for him. Yeah, we all know about that. That's a good one. Like in *Jackie Brown*, when you see the close-up of Bridget Fonda's feet. I guess he'll just throw the feet in there wherever he sees fit.

I think there's an honesty and a general forthrightness in his work and he doesn't apologize for it. Even if he's wrong. I think he shoots straight. Like the use of the "n" word, which we all know about. That's not something he used in his own life. I mean, that's not done. But if he felt it needed to be used in a scene, he used it without apologizing for it. So in that sense, I think Quentin is really doing what he believes. What he wants to do. He has a vision, I think. Sometimes he's more successful than others, but I do think he still has that. He's still honestly trying to say whatever it is he wants to say.

DON MURPHY

Don Murphy is a name that is sure to be familiar to fans of Quentin Tarantino. Murphy and former partner Jane Hamsher produced *Natural Born Killers*. Through a long, complicated chain of events, Tarantino and Murphy would become enemies. Murphy once commented that he would publicly celebrate Tarantino's death. An angry Tarantino confronted Murphy in a pricey Los Angeles restaurant and the two ensued in an altercation. Tarantino would then announce on national television that he had "bitch slapped" Murphy. This comment would lead to a $5 million lawsuit by Murphy against the director. (It would later be dropped.)

Knowing all of this, I approached this interview with Murphy very cautiously. I decided I would keep the conversation away from Tarantino and anything remotely controversial. I would instead focus solely on *Natural Born Killers* and *My Best Friend's Birthday*, which has also been optioned by the producer. To my surprise, Tarantino and Murphy had spoken since the lawsuit had been dropped and squashed their differences.

Murphy's other production credits include *Shoot 'Em Up*, *Real Steel*, and *Transformers*.

What elements of Natural Born Killers *initially attracted you to the screenplay?*

It said a lot about where society was at that point, in regards to fame and in regards to the public. At the same time, it could be done for a price. You know? It could be done for a million dollars if you'd wanted it to. Quentin had designed it to be all handheld.

Aside from Rand Vossler and Oliver Stone, a number of directors flirted with Natural Born Killers. *Could you tell me about some of them?*

There was a moment there after Rand Vossler when we tried to explore the idea with Al Magnoli. At a certain point, his representatives wanted us to sort of give it to him without any promises that the film would get made. We declined to do so. There was a moment there when a company named CB Pictures, a French company which has gone belly-up, a man named Paul Felter wanted to make *Natural Born Killers* and he wanted his friend Sean Penn to direct it. We met with Sean, and it was never really very clear just how serious Sean was about it and so we didn't pursue that. There was a gentleman named Mark Rocco, who went on to direct *Murder in the First*, who wanted to direct it. But we were interested in making it. We met with Mark. We thought Mark had a great vision for it, but I didn't know how he intended to get it financed. So we didn't pursue that.

When Oliver Stone first signed on to do Natural Born Killers, *what was your initial reaction?*

That he was full of shit.

Okay, once you realized that he was seriously interested in the project, what was your reaction?

I was relieved, I was in awe, and I was quite pleased because I really thought he had a handle on the material and I really knew it was going to get made. I believed that we were gonna survive as producers, too, which was what we really wanted to do. We wanted to make the film.

Stone has his share of critics, and say what you will, but he is a filmmaker who definitely has a passion for his work.

He's probably the only person who could have got that film made at the studio level. Quite possibly the only person.

I understand the Natural Born Killers *shoot was quite interesting. What was the strangest thing you saw on the entire shoot?*

The strangest thing I saw on the whole shoot? People come out from miles around in Winslow, Arizona to take up picnic baskets and sit up on the hills and watch us basically stage an elaborate shootout in a drug store till like five in the morning. You know the scene where he's in the drug store?

Yeah.

And the windows are all getting blown out, right?

Yeah.

Well, those windows got blown out like twenty times. And you'd have to go back and reset them and everything else. And these people came and sat through all of that. There must have been like a hundred people. And they sat so far back, I don't know what they could see anyway. But it was like, *Wow! We're the entertainment for the night.* How strange.

Woody Harrelson and Juliette Lewis' characters were supposed to be passionately in love, but in real-life, they didn't get along. Were you ever afraid that would affect their performances, and do you think to any degree that it did?

No. I was never afraid. They were professionals. In my opinion, as far as the film goes, no. I think they look like they are in love, and that's for you to decide if you think I'm wrong.

I understand Stone's initial cut was quite different from the version released. Your former partner Jane Hamsher called it "completely unintelligible." What were some of the differences in that first cut?

I wouldn't agree that it was completely unintelligible. I think that was my ex-partner's opinion. I think that what Oliver had tried to do was be so experimental that the first cut completely avoided almost any sense of linearity, which while it may have been a more daring way to go in some reality, for the film, you really—unless you knew what the story was going into—you had no idea what the hell was going on. But I think that was a choice that Oliver consciously made, and the film that came out represented what Oliver wanted released. I think that first screening may have been part of Oliver's master plan to kind of throw everybody off guard, to be honest with you.

What is your assessment of the final film?

I'd like to almost parrot back what Oliver said to me once, which I agreed with. It's the kind of film that, like *Clockwork Orange*, I hope its reputation builds over years. Every time you see it, there's more in it. More technique. He put so much technique into it. He put so much style into it, which the original script never really called for. The script just calls for a handheld camera. You know, he spent the $40 million really well. I can't really look at it objectively because it made my career. But it's certainly a film that had I not made it, I would still want to see.

You've also optioned My Best Friend's Birthday, *which was written by Quentin Tarantino and Craig Hamann. What are some elements of that screenplay that interest you?*

The comedies that I like best, be it the *Heathers*, or whatever, are just over the top. Over the top with a real sense of humor. And it was written by them [Tarantino and Hamann] to make a modern-day screwball comedy, which still hasn't been done in a long time. I mean, *The Waterboy* and all this other crap out there is really not a modern-day screwball comedy, which is what this is. It's like circumstance leads to circumstance leads to circumstance.

A little over a year has passed since your incident with Quentin Tarantino. What is your take on all that today?

I think whenever people get successful, be it the huge, unbelievable success that Quentin received, or the modest success that my ex-partner Jane and I received, or the minor success a new actor on a TV show receives, I think the really important thing is to not take anything too seriously. And I would say that everybody involved in the Quentin saga, including myself, Quentin, and Jane and Oliver [Stone], Craig [Hamann], Cathryn [Jaymes], Roger [Avary], everybody really took everything too seriously, looking back on it. And there really was no chance of a reproach as long as everybody was doing that. Now, over a year later, I look back on that, and that's what I think.

I had a chance to talk with Quentin at the New Line Christmas party, and it was a peaceful talk. You know, I think he's an immensely-talented filmmaker and I wish him nothing but continued success, just like I wish everybody—from myself to Jane to Oliver—continued success. What I find interesting looking back on it is that nobody, myself included, behaved in a way to be proud of.

P.J. PESCE

Miami screenwriter/director P.J. Pesce studied directing under the tutelage of famed filmmakers Martin Scorsese and Brian De Palma. In 1994, he made his feature directorial debut with the Sam Elliott-starrer *The Desperate Trail*, which *Entertainment Weekly* called "The best Western on any sized screen since *Unforgiven*." Based on his work on that film, executive producers Quentin Tarantino and Robert Rodriguez tapped Pesce to helm the prequel to their film *From Dusk Till Dawn* with *From Dusk Till Dawn 3: The Hangman's Daughter*. The film would ultimately become Dimension Pictures' highest-grossing direct-to-video film to date.

Other Pesce-directed films include *Sniper 3, The Lost Boys: The Tribe,* and *Smokin' Aces 2: Assassin's Ball.*

How did you become involved with From Dusk Till Dawn 3: The Hangman's Daughter?

I had made *The Desperate Trail*. At the time I was writing this movie, *The Battle of Ono*, for Chow Yun Fat, Terrence Chang, and John Woo. The original idea was that it would be Fat's first American film. There's a well-known Asian director named King Hoo who, for ten years, had been trying to make *The Battle of Ono*. It looked like they had finally gotten it together because of Chow Yun Fat's new-found popularity in the West, but then King Hoo died before they could begin shooting. And Terrence and John, as well as Hoo I guess, all loved *The Desperate Trail*, so they had me working on this script. So, unbeknownst to me, the search for this prequel was kind of a big deal, and all these young directors in Hollywood wanted to do it. Then my agent sent me the script, and I thought it was really funny. Really cool. I loved *From Dusk Till Dawn*, but I was just concentrating on writing at that time. So I wasn't really putting any effort into it, which was probably the best thing I could have done. They said, "Oh, can you be around to talk to Robert Rodriguez on the phone?" I was like, "Yeah, sure."

So Robert and I got on the phone and, I don't know, we just really hit it off. We both just started talking about movies. We talked about the script a little bit, but we talked more about other stuff; just like each other, and what we liked to do. A few days later, my agent asked if I could get on a plane to Austin. And I was like, "Oh, shit! My band is playing tomorrow night. I need to rehearse. Can I do it the day after tomorrow?" He was like, "What are you, an idiot? Robert Rodriguez wants you to go down and talk to him." So I went down and saw Robert and we basically talked about the same things. I went to his house and met his wife, Elizabeth, and their babies. And Robert and I just kind of ran around like idiots—played the guitar, played on the computer, looked at some stuff he'd shot for *Road Racers* and, I don't know, after maybe four hours of this, he turns to me and says, "So how would you like to shoot this movie?" [Laughs.] I was like, "Oh, I don't know. I might do it like this. . . ." And we talked about *The Desperate Trail*, which he had seen.

I think it really came down to two things—Quentin and Robert really liked *The Desperate Trail*, and Robert and I just really hit it off. We just really liked each other. I think he's just sort of a regular guy. It made it all very easy. A couple of days later, I got word that I had the job. And from there it went very quickly. I was casting and went off to South Africa to scout, and then we went off and made the movie in September. I think it was the first of July when I had met Robert, and then two months later I was away filming. It was really fucked up because I went through— they say the five most stressful things you can do are take on a new job, get an operation, go through a divorce, move, or buy a house. I was operated on for a double hernia. I started a new job, which was making this movie. I bought a house and I moved. I was more exhausted starting this movie than I had ever been finishing a movie. But that was the beginning of *From Dusk Till Dawn 3*.

Did you feel any pressure working in the shadow of Robert Rodriguez?

No, I really didn't. Robert is really supportive as a fellow filmmaker. And when you're working—when I'm working, anyway—you're under so much pressure that you don't have time to think about things like that. You just have to do what you do. If it's anything, now I think, *Geez, he's ripping off Robert's style*, when really my style is just really similar to his anyway. You know, the sort of very quick cutting and such.

Michael Parks is great. Was there any hesitation to cast him since he'd already appeared as a different character in the first installment of From Dusk Till Dawn*?*

No, no. There were some concerns because Michael had a really difficult reputation from the past. So I just said, "Let's go meet with him." Quentin was just adamant. "You've got to, got to, got to cast Michael Parks!" So I just said, "Let me meet him first. Let the decision be mine." And they were very generous about that.

Michael came in and we met. He was very wary. I don't think he liked the idea that he had to come in and meet with me. But he subsequently came over to my house and we got really fucking drunk as hell. [Laughs.] We drank a whole bottle of brandy. Then I broke out the guitar and started playing, and Michael just had this amazing voice. You know, years before he had actually cut a record. Apparently, and I didn't know this, but apparently he sang the theme song to the TV show *Then Came Bronson* he was on. We just had a pretty good time together.

You went back and re-shot the ending of the film. Could you tell me a little bit about the original ending and why it wasn't used?

Well, the original story was just like, it was an attempt to mimic an Ambrose Bierce short story, where everybody dies, and you cut very quickly and you're in a bar and it's a guy telling you this story. And the guy he's telling this story to is me, and I'm saying, "Oh, that's bullshit. That's the stupidest thing I ever heard!" And the camera slowly moves around and you realize the guy telling me the story is Michael Parks. And then he rips out my heart and kills me, and you realize that he's a vampire. So it's sort of one of those O. Henry-type endings, which a lot of Ambrose Bierce's macabre stories had similar kind of endings. Well, the problem was, when we screened it for an audience, the fucking audience was furious with us. You know, you can't do that. You ripped them off! And the real problem that we realized when we screened it was that none of the dramatic tensions that we had set up in the body of the movie were in any way answered. So that, I think, was the biggest problem; like both Johnny Madrid, who's the hero, and Ambrose Bierce, who's Michael Parks, are killed. Several of the bad guys—the key vampires—just disappear, and you're left wondering what happened to them. And the hangman doesn't really have any kind of ending. You know, that's it. We all talked about it afterwards and I sort of went off and thought about it, and I realized, you just have to ask the questions you always ask as a writer, like, "What are the tensions in the movie?" and "What are the different ways they could play out?" So, actually my editor, Larry Maddox, came up with some of the greatest ideas that I wound up using. And I went off and wrote it, showed it to everybody, and they all dug it, and we went off for three days and shot it.

So the original ending was, you never got outside of the bar. And the ending now is much, much more satisfying. You've got Marco and Michael Parks outside, and then Marco goes off with Michael Parks to join Pancho Villa.

What was Robert Rodriguez and Quentin Tarantino's involvement with the film?

Quentin was really much more involved with Scott Spiegel's movie. With our movie, Quentin's major involvement was talking to me before we got started—talking about casting Michael Parks. Robert was involved with me. I mean, Robert and I spoke three or four times a day until I went to South Africa. All during the casting process. It was the first time he'd ever produced anything for anyone else, and I have to say, he did a really great job. He became my friend and my protector and my producer in the best sense of the word. He would say things like, "You know, I think you're doing yourself a disservice here. You should do this like this. . . ." He was kind of my guide through Miramax. He also just became a fellow director I respected. I could just ask him his thoughts on anything. That was tremendous.

And once I went to South Africa, I spoke to Robert once a day, or I e-mailed him, you know, pretty much every day until we started shooting. And once I started shooting, everybody just left me alone and let me do my job.

Are you a fan of Tarantino's work?

I am, yeah.

As a filmmaker, what do you think are his strengths?

I think the most obvious thing to say is that Quentin has an amazing sense of dialogue, of naturalism, sense of realism, and yet he knows how to make that interesting narratively. In every scene. He got a great deal of that, I think, from Howard Hawks, in that every scene begins with a question you want answered desperately as an audience member. That said, I think he also has an ability to take outlandish movie situations and make them feel completely real. Like it's your friends up there in *Reservoir Dogs*. They're people that you know or have met at a party, you know what I mean? It's not like some fucking guy in an Armani suit. No. It's like a bunch of fucking guys that you know. Some guy that fucking dealt pot in high school like Mr. Pink. We fuckin' know that guy. I mean, all of those guys, really. Fuckin' Chris Penn when he's truckin' down the fuckin' boulevard with his Adidas suit on, talkin' on the phone to Daddy. We know that fat spoiled brat from the suburbs. That was the most striking thing to me the first time I saw it. I was like, *Oh, my God! This feels so much more real than any heist movie I've ever seen.*

And the other thing I think Quentin is highly underrated for is just the way he stages shots. I mean visually, the way he uses actors—moves them around with the shot and allows the actors to act without cutting, is a really highly-underrated skill. Most American actors don't do that, myself included. I would like to get better at doing that. I just came from seeing Frank Whaley's movie *Joe the King* at Sundance, and he's got shots that go on for six or seven minutes. And it's not like the camera just stays still.

By the way, here's another interesting little story. So Frank, who plays Brett in *Pulp Fiction*—I've always taken credit for Frank getting that part. What happened was this: When *Reservoir Dogs* first came out, some people knew about it, but not everybody did. It wasn't like Quentin is now, where everybody knows him and he's like an international fucking superstar. After *Reservoir Dogs* came out, you know, like a couple of people knew about it. It was more of a cult thing. So Frank is out here from New York and we're hanging out. One day he and his girlfriend are at my house, and I'm like, "Dude, you've gotta watch this movie. It's great." We stay up and watch it on laserdisc, and they're like, "Wow, that was really good. I dug that movie." So, I don't know, maybe three or four weeks go by and I get this call from Frank. He says, "Listen, you know that guy whose movie we watched? Well, they offered me a part in his next movie and I'm thinking about doing it." And I'm like, "Well fuck, man, you've got to do it. I think this guy's gonna be really big." I'd already read the script, too, and I thought it was gonna be great. And he was like, "I don't know. They're not gonna give me single-card billing and they're not gonna do this," and I was just like, "Who gives a fuck, man?" And he was like, "No, no, you gotta pay attention to that shit." So I got off the phone, and he sounded like he wasn't going to do it. So two days go by and I'd keep thinking, "Fucking Whaley is screwing up here. He's really screwing up." So finally I just called him and left a message on his machine. I said, "Franko, it's Pesce, listen. I don't know if I'm out of line here, but with all due respect, I think you should really do that movie that Tarantino guy is doing. I just think you should do it. Fuck that credit shit. This movie's gonna be big. He's gonna be big. I just think you should do it." And that was it. I don't hear from him. Two days go by. Three days go by. Fuckin' four days go by, and Frank is like a fuckin' temperamental actor sometimes, you know? *And I'm like, Fuck, did I offend him now?* So on the fifth day I get a call from Whaley and he's like, "I took your advice. I took the part." And I was like, "Oh, excellent!" And he says, "Um, so what days are *The Desperate Trail* shooting?" And I was like, *oh no, he's taken this movie I told him he should take and now he won't be able to do my movie.* But thankfully it worked out. He actually came right from shooting *Pulp Fiction* to our set in Santa Fe to do *The Desperate Trail*. I had to remind him of that this weekend. I'm sure all the residual checks he's gotten from the movie. . . . [Laughs.]

He was great in Pulp Fiction.

He's pretty fuckin' hysterical in that. Whaley is my brother, and he's the fuckin' shit. We've been through some shit together. I was so glad to have him with me on *The Desperate Trail*.

Which of Tarantino's films is your favorite?

Reservoir Dogs is still my favorite because I think the writing, the acting, and the casting is so perfect. I don't believe there's one wrong move in that movie. I could just watch that again and again.

TOM SAVINI

Tom Savini is well known to cineastes around the globe as the "king of splatter." Savini's track record is an impressive one. Of course Tarantino fans identify Savini as the character Sex Machine in *From Dusk Till Dawn*. Other notable acting appearances include *Dawn of the Dead*, *Two Evil Eyes*, and The Creep in *Creepshow 2*. In addition to this, he is also the special-effects makeup wizard behind *Friday the 13th's* Jason Voorhees, as well as tons of other notable films, including the Tarantino-produced *Killing Zoe*. Savini is also a talented filmmaker in his own right. In 1990, he helmed the impressive remake of George Romero's *Night of the Living Dead*.

In 2007, Savini was cast as a bumbling deputy in the Tarantino/Robert Rodriguez team-up *Grindhouse*. Savini has since reunited with Tarantino in *Django Unchained*, in which he appeared as a tracker.

I recently read that Tarantino once approached you at a convention and asked you to make an appearance at Video Archives, the video store where he was employed. Is that true?

No, it wasn't a public appearance. He had come to me, "Mr. Savini, I'm a big fan of yours. I work in this video store." I was out in L.A. at this convention. He said, "It's in Manhattan Beach and it would be great if you came by because we have a lot of old movies. We have most of your movies." And I went by. He might have had *Reservoir Dogs* in the back room. I don't know. But I went and I chatted with him. I saw him at a party at [KNB Efx wiz] Greg Nicotero's house later. Then, shortly after that, he became Quentin Tarantino.

What was your impression of him the first time you met?

He was working in the video store and he did know a lot about movies. He knew everything that was on the shelf. He knew what they had and what they were about, but I was just visiting there and maybe signing a couple of films. I mean, he was just a fan back then. Then when I saw him at the party, he wasn't talking very much. So I always regret not talking to him very much, because I love talking to people who are into movies and are aware. But I don't remember doing that with him at that party. I remember talking to him on the set of *Killing Zoe*, which he produced. And it was only then that we talked a lot and he told me that he thought I was great in *Knightriders*. He said, "Your performance in that film was so real. You were great in that!" You know how Quentin talks.

Yeah.

You know, "you were great in that." In my subconscious I'm thinking, *Well, if you thought that, why didn't you cast me for Reservoir Dogs?* You know? But then again, I live in Pittsburgh and you know, if you're gonna do a low-budget film in LA, you're gonna need local actors. As an actor, you're always thinking about the next job, so I remember thinking that. But I enjoyed talking with him on the set of *Killing Zoe* because he was saying things to his friend Roger Avary like, "Hey, Roger, look! You got Tom Savini on your crew!" They made me feel like they were still fans and that they appreciated me and had grown up watching my films.

As I'm sure you've heard by now, Quentin once lied on his résumé and listed himself as one of the bikers from Dawn of the Dead. *Do you remember seeing him there? [Laughs.]*

No. [Laughs.] Quentin was not in *Dawn of the Dead*. You know what? It's so true that lots of people lie on their résumés. I mean, I have had people bring their résumés to me and they've had my films on them, as far as doing makeup effects. And I don't like that. My résumé, which is three pages long, is absolutely true. In fact, I would love to put a big header on there on the bottom of it, you know: "The preceding material is absolutely true one hundred percent," you know? Because it's so common that people lie on their résumés. With my stuff, it looks like I'm lying. Here I am, a combat photographer in Vietnam, a certified fight director with the Society of British Fight Directors, a tournament fencer, a bullwhip expert.... I mean, If I read that, I'd think it was bullshit! But it's true. Unfortunately, Hollywood frowns on versatility. When I grew up, my dad was a plumber, an electrician, a carpenter, a mason—he could build anything—he was a shoemaker. He fixed our shoes for us and made us toys. My dad could do anything. So me growing up as a photographer, a stunt guy, as an actor, director, makeup effects, sculpting. I always thought the more you do, the more you will get to do. You know? That's been my philosophy. But people just don't believe you can be good at a lot of things. And it's absolutely true. My dad is a prime example of that, and I hope that I am.

How did you become involved with From Dusk Till Dawn?

I got a phone call from casting people about an audition. They wanted me to come out there and I couldn't do it, so I said I'd send them an audition tape. This was on a Friday. They said they would FedEx me the script. But the tape had to be in by the following Friday. One week. Well, I'm waiting and waiting, and the script's never coming! The script arrived Thursday! This was the day before I was supposed to have the tape in! So I had no time to memorize the lines, so I wrote the lines on cards and threw them around my bedroom and set up my video camera. This had to be FedEx-ed that day! So I set up the video camera, grabbed a costume, and did all kinds of shit, which worked because in reading the lines, it looked like I was looking at different people while I was talking. So that kind of worked. But I wrote the lines on these cards and set them behind the video camera, made the tape, and sent it off. And then I heard that Quentin liked me. They asked me to fly out for a costume fitting, and I did. And then I came back and I worked out like crazy and I lost a lot of weight, got my abs back, built my body up, and in six weeks went out and started shooting.

You were originally approached to play Frost instead of Sex Machine. Is that right?

Yeah, that's true. In fact, Sex Machine is a big guy and Frost is a little guy. But when I read the script, I said, "This Sex Machine character is a lot more interesting." So the audition tape that I sent was for Sex Machine. I didn't even read Frost's lines. From what I understand, I made Quentin laugh, and he switched the body types and gave me Sex Machine.

I had read that you were responsible for expanding the scene where Sex Machine fights off the vampires Jackie Chan-style with the broken pool cue. Is this true?

Well, like I said, I'm a certified fight director, and I knew the stunt guys 'cause they were all from *Knightriders*. And they worked real close with me to make sure I did the backflip off the pool table. I did all that stuff! The only thing I did not do was fly through the window when all the bats came in. That was gonna involve an air ramp and all that. I did the fights. All the fights and, like I said, the backflip myself. And I suggested the bullwhip because, you know, I'm pretty good with a bullwhip. And that became part of my character. But also when I creep up behind Fred Williamson, you know, Robert wanted me to just jump up and bite him in the neck. I said, "Hey, look at these long fingernails here. How about if you just see them first, almost like they're spiders? Then I jump up and bite him." He goes, "Let me see it." Then I did it, and he shot seven takes. That was my contribution to the movie. It happens all the time. And I suggested things to Juliette Lewis, whom I was afraid of. I had just seen her in *Natural Born Killers*, and she could kick ass! But she was in character all the time as the seventeen-year-old little girl and it was great. So I suggested things like, "How about when we're walking, I say, 'Hi, I'm Sex Machine' and I grab your hand and we shake hands real quick." And she said, "Yeah, yeah, great, great, great!" And then, off camera, she said, "You know, I've seen you before. You're good." And I'm thinking, *Where in the hell would she have seen me?* Maybe I looked like somebody she had seen, but I thanked her and was honored that she would say that because I think she's just the greatest. But I was intimidated by her.

But that happens all the time. You suggest things back and forth, you know, and a good director—and Robert is a good director—listens to everybody. The craft service people, the P.A.s; listens to everybody, but then just chooses the good stuff he wants to use. I try to do that. I listen to everybody, but I make it clear that I choose the things that I like that I hear. I don't like everything, you know? But you allow everybody to talk and to make suggestions. So that happens all the time.

On a similar note, I heard that you were responsible for Sex Machine's using the crotch gun from Desperado *and that Robert hadn't intended to use it.*

No. Actually, the crotch gun was a big surprise to me. I didn't even know I was gonna wear that until the day they brought it out. And I just laughed hysterically because I knew my friends were gonna see this, you know, and I could just imagine the kind of crap I was gonna get. But I had no idea. I heard later on that he couldn't get the crotch gun to work in *Desperado*, but he did get it to work on *From Dusk Till Dawn*, and I was lucky enough to have worn it.

I've heard it was a pretty fun shoot.

It was a dream come true. You know how you have a dream about winning the lottery or finding this buried treasure and you wake up and you're all pissed off that it's not true? I was afraid I was gonna wake up and not really be there.

How would you describe the atmosphere? It looks like it was pretty loose. I've seen pictures of Robert Rodriguez playing the guitar on set.

Yeah, between takes he would play the guitar. It was just so much fun. There was always something new. Every corner you walked around, there were so many people involved in the cast and the fight scenes that outside there were guys singing and playing the guitar. People playing cards in horrible makeup. People carrying limbs to the set. And the effects shop was right there in the studio with Greg Nicotero, my ex-protégé. I got to hang out there with Salma Hayek. I was shooting videos of everything constantly, of Salma Hayek. There's a close-up of the fangs in her mouth and she's saying, "Kiss me, darling." I'll always regret not kissing her. My daughter was learning Spanish from the costume people and martial arts from the stunt guys. She was painting hands for the special effects guys. It was just like a fantastic eight-week dream come true.

What did you think of the final film?

I loved it, but I thought it was too short. I thought it ended too abruptly. Too soon.

As a filmmaker yourself, what is your opinion of Quentin Tarantino?

With Quentin, his bravery is impressive. His visual style is also impressive. But the main thing that I always say about Quentin is that what impresses me and what is unique about him is that he violates story structure. It's almost like he writes every scene on a stack of index cards, throws them into the air, lets them hit the ground, and whatever way he picks them up, that's the way the movie's gonna go! [Laughs.] No, it's a little more structured than that, but it seems that way. It's so scattered. I mean, look at the brilliant editing of *Pulp Fiction*, jumping back and forth like that. I mean, if you shot that in continuity it would not be the same. It wouldn't be that interesting at all. You know, John Travolta would get killed after all that wonderful stuff.

The film almost makes you believe it has a happy ending. Because of the non-linear structure, we're almost able to forget that Travolta is dead as we see them leaving the diner at the end of the film.

Exactly. The film would have been so different if you'd had all those wonderful things with Sam Jackson and then, suddenly, Travolta is killed so quickly, so haphazardly. But you're right. And it's the editing. That's where Quentin's brilliance lies. He's just incredible, and I really respect someone like that, who thinks that way. Watching one of his films is like going to the latest exhibit by an artist.

TONY SCOTT

Before Tarantino's success, Tony Scott was one of his favorite filmmakers. Tarantino especially loved *Revenge,* which starred Kevin Costner and Anthony Quinn. So, when Scott signed on to direct his screenplay for *True Romance,* Tarantino was overjoyed. Tony Scott would ultimately make some changes, but Tarantino would support the film and remain good friends with him up until Scott's death in 2012. Tarantino would also perform a rewrite for Scott's film, *Crimson Tide.*

In addition to these projects, Tarantino and Scott also cooked up a proposed adaptation of Elmore Leonard's novel *Killshot* in the late 1990s, which would have starred Tarantino and Robert De Niro. However, this collaboration never wound up happening, and *Killshot* was instead made with John Madden at the helm in 2008.

True Romance *is an interesting film because there are no clear-cut "good guys." Clarence and Alabama are definitely anti-heroes.*

You know, that was Quentin's first screenplay, and to be honest, I hold him responsible for the uniqueness of the characters in *Crimson Tide.* You know, he came in and did a rewrite. We all loved the story, but we weren't sure about the characters until Quentin came in and rewrote them completely.

The best script I've ever had, which barely changed from the moment it hit my desk to the point the movie was finished, was *True Romance.* I'm not just saying that because it was Quentin, either. It was brilliant. The characters were so full and so well-drawn that it makes a director's life so much easier when you can go to the set and put your hand on your chest and say, "This fuckin' scene is brilliant. You guys are doing this scene and there's no variation here." And every actor just wanted to come to the set and do the words that were there on the page, you know? I can't remember one day where I struggled with an actor who wanted to change things. Everyday they came to work saying, "This is great!"

The scene in between Christopher Walken and Dennis Hopper is easily one of the decade's most memorable. Did you know at the time how special that scene was?

I knew it was brilliant when I read it on the page. The first time I read it, I just died laughing. I read that in a little hotel in Italy at 3 a.m. while I was on the road shooting. I said, "This scene is brilliant." It's kind of funny because, even though I wanted to make this movie great, it was actually one of the easiest two days' shooting of my career. The scene was so well written, so well crafted, and the actors were so good that I didn't have to move the camera because I had total confidence in them, just letting them run it. The camera was a "lock off" and I just let them do it, and I think it turned out great.

You had a remarkable cast. When you have Sam Jackson, Gary Oldman, Brad Pitt, and Val Kilmer playing bit parts, you know you've got an incredibly strong cast.

When you have good material, every actor wants to do it. They all did it for scale. I let both Gary and Brad run with their characters. Gary said, "I've got a vision about who this guy is." He was just finishing a movie, and there was this guy hanging around the set who was a Jamaican drug dealer who'd been living in New York for fifteen years. So he said, "This is the guy!" That was his idea. The same with Brad. He said, "This is one of my roommates!" [Laughs.]

How much of the scene with Samuel L. Jackson was cut from the final version of the film?

The first scene in the hotel room? Not really that much.

[Producer] Bill Unger told me that you sustained a prop gun injury while you were shooting True Romance. *What happened?*

Chris Walken puts the gun to Dennis Hopper's forehead, or at least he was originally supposed to, just before he kills him. We were rehearsing it and when Chris went to pull the trigger, Dennis said, "Fuck that! I don't like this idea! This is scary shit! This is too close to home." [Laughs.] I said, "Listen, Dennis, I'll fucking do it!" I said I'd rehearse it and I'd do it. Well, the gun was one where it had a slide, and the slide came out about a quarter of an inch and it punctured a perfect hole in my forehead.

Another story I've heard is that you originally intended for Christian Slater to emulate Quentin. Fact or myth?

No. That's just a myth.

Neither Elvis Presley's name nor his music wound up in the film. Was there a conflict with the estate?

The estate didn't want us to use it because they'd read the script and they thought there was too much violence. They didn't want the king's name attached to a movie that had so much violence in it.

Who came up with the title "Mentor" for that character?

That was my idea, I think. [Laughs.] There was really no choice since we couldn't use the name.

It was still rather obvious who it was.

Yeah, it was obvious. Val was rather brilliant. He's such a freak. He's so great! [Laughs.]

True Romance—both Quentin's script and the final film—seemed to have been very much influenced by Terrence Malick's Badlands.

Badlands is one of my favorite movies. I think *True Romance* was a tribute to *Badlands*, and I didn't try to disguise the fact. I loved the script for *True Romance*, and I loved *Badlands*, and I thought, *Here is a way to pay tribute.* I've done that before in other films, such as *Enemy of the State*, which was a tribute to *The Conversation.*

Tarantino has many different talents. What do you think is his strength?

First writing, second directing, and third acting. You know, *Killshot* was gonna be a double act with Bob [De Niro] and Quentin. That was the perfect role for Quentin.

Was he gonna play Richie Nix?

Yeah. You've read the book?

Yeah, I'm a huge fan of Elmore Leonard's work.

What's funny is that, in the book, the woman comes through in the end. This would be completely different from what Quentin's done in the past. It becomes her. She becomes the hero. It completely becomes her movie. [Editor's note: This interview was conducted before *Kill Bill*.]

That would be interesting, considering the flak he got about Reservoir Dogs *not having any women in there.*

This is completely the other way around. It's great.

What's the current status of Killshot?

I think it's actually in a stalemate position because Quentin is off doing his own thing. I loved it and I still do. I don't know where it still stands because he was gonna come in and do a final polish on the screenplay. That never happened because he got buried doing his own thing.

What does the first draft look like?

The first draft was great, but there's the machinations of the deal and who owns it. I'm not prepared to walk away from my own company to do it for someone else.

Is De Niro still interested in the project?

He loves it still.

What's your take on Quentin Tarantino and Roger Avary's now infamous dissertation on the "homosexual subtext" of Top Gun?

I pissed myself laughing! [Laughs.] I thought it was brilliant. He called me up and said, "You ought to look at this before it comes out." I thought it was brilliant. I haven't spoken to Quentin in a while, but he's a brilliant writer and quite a visionary. Not in big ways, just in small ways. He just makes people live and breathe in a way that no one else has brought to the cinema in a long, long time.

Something kind of funny regarding Quentin's Top Gun *analysis is that now there's a similar theory based on* Reservoir Dogs. *[Laughs.] They've said that there was homosexual subtext there! Have you heard that?*

No! I'd be really interested to hear what Quentin's got to say about that.

SCOTT SPIEGEL

Birmingham, Michigan screenwriter/director/actor Scott Spiegel began his career as a part of a group which also included Sam Raimi and Bruce Campbell. Together, the group made numerous short films before they made *The Evil Dead*. In 1987, Spiegel co-wrote the follow-up to that film, *Evil Dead 2*. In 1989, he made his directorial debut with *Intruder*. The following year, he co-wrote the Clint Eastwood vehicle *The Rookie*.

In the late 1980s, Spiegel befriended a would-be filmmaker named Quentin Tarantino, introducing him to a number of important people and thus giving his career a major assist. Returning the favor, Tarantino later hired Spiegel to write and direct the 1999 film *From Dusk Till Dawn 2: Texas Blood Money*, which he executive produced. Tarantino also produced Spiegel's third directorial effort, an adaptation of Peter O'Donnell's novel *Modesty Blaise* (coincidentally the novel Vincent is reading when he's gunned down in *Pulp Fiction*).

The following interview was conducted just before the release of *From Dusk Till Dawn 2*.

How did you become involved with From Dusk Till Dawn 2*?*

Quentin and I went to see *From Dusk Till Dawn* at the Cinerama Dome for a midnight show. The first night it opened, we met Bob Weinstein there, and he says, "Wait. Why don't we get Scott to direct the sequel?" And Quentin said, "Yeah, great idea!" So that's basically how it all came about.

I've read that there was an early draft of the screenplay in which Seth and Richie Gecko appear in the film. Could you tell me a little bit about that, and why it got scrapped?

Basically that idea was discarded because of Quentin. I don't think he wanted to do it. He's taking the whole acting thing very seriously right now, you know, and he's got a different point of view on it. He didn't want to reprise his role, but basically that was the pitch that pretty much landed me the deal. I came up with—well, me and Boaz Yakin, a fellow filmmaker—a story that basically picks up after the first film, where George Clooney's just off in his car and he's got all the dough. He's going to hook up with another band of criminals. Theoretically it would have been Seth and Richie. Then they would put that money towards a bigger job and, you know, rob the bank and retire. But, of course, Seth doesn't make it too far, and the police gun him down. The guys hear about it, get wind of this on the news, and they figure, "Well, that explains Seth, but where the hell is Richie?" They figure their last stop was the Titty Twister, so they go back there, this whole new gang of criminal-types who happen to know Seth and Richie. They go to track down Richie at the Titty Twister, and Richie's in the back room somewhere, and he's looking weird. He's kind of in the shadows, you know? And you would basically learn that Richie's the new head of the vampire clan at the Titty Twister. And then all hell breaks loose and you kind of have a mini-battle, kind of like what you had in the first *From Dusk Till Dawn*. The guys escape, but of course one of them gets bitten, and they still can't believe these are really vampires. They go off and go to a bank job and, one by one, you know: this one guy who was bitten infects everyone else.

So basically Quentin came on as an uncredited writer and reworked the first act with me. We made it more like *The Magnificent Seven* or whatever, where you've got these guys who all have to work together to pull a job. So some things were very much reworked. It would have been kind of cool to have seen that movie.

Bob Weinstein even said, "Yeah, we could get George Clooney to do a cameo," and all that stuff. I think price-wise it may have been cost prohibitive. But I liked the way Quentin turned it out, but I think Bob Weinstein liked the direction I had been going in, so that caused kind of a weird problem, but we worked it all out nonetheless.

Duane Whitaker did some writing, as well.

Yeah, that was Quentin's idea. I had known Duane for several years, but we had never worked together before. Quentin showed me this film called *Stripteaser* that Duane had written. We watched that, and we were laughing. And Quentin says, "Why don't you guys write the screenplay together?" So I was like, "Cool." And Duane would also co-star in the film. So that was kind of the deal, and I'm glad Duane brought all kinds of whacked-out characterizations and weird lines and stuff to the script. It was really cool working with him.

In this film, you got to work briefly with your old pal Bruce Campbell again. What's Bruce like to work with?

We've just been working together forever. There's just so much stuff that goes unsaid. He knows what I want and he knows what I'm going for. It's just weird. He's great. Lots of laughs. He's like the total professional. He knows how to do everything, so I designed a sequence for him to do in reverse motion. Just a portion of a little scene, and he just knows everything. It's cool because it's kind of a cameo in the beginning of the film. I wish it was more, but it worked out perfectly for his schedule. Bruce is just great. I was very lucky to have him.

Quentin is a big Bruce Campbell fan. What did he have to say about Bruce appearing in the film?

Actually, it was Quentin's idea. I didn't know. I was hoping to get Bruce somewhere in that movie, but depending on all the scheduling and all that stuff. And then it was Quentin's idea for him to be the guy at the beginning of the movie. I went, "Yeah! Fucking-A right!" Most of the casting choices—Bo Hopkins and

Duane Whitaker and people like that—were Quentin's ideas. So that was pretty cool.

How in the world did Tiffani Amber Thiessen become involved with the film?

I know, it's weird. Well, there was a whole list of having those, you know, kind of Drew Barrymore/*Scream*-type fake-outs in this movie. Actually, Heather Locklear really wanted to do it, but basically, she owes her soul to Aaron Spelling. So she sent us a nice letter saying, "I really wanna do this, you guys. It's just that I can't get out of this prior commitment." And who can blame her? She's great. Actually, she auditioned for me on another project. So I guess they said, "Look, we'll find somebody." I really had nothing to do with it, obviously, other than saying, "Yeah, she's great. Let's get her." And what a pro Tiffani is, because we were tormenting her with phony bats and cramming them in her mouth and up her skirt! [Laughs.] She was just a great sport. She was really cool. She had a great sense of humor, and she got along great with Bruce. I guess it was just our casting director Marsha Shulman and Miramax putting something together to kind of make that happen. But Tiffani's cool. She definitely has a following, as does Bruce.

Once shooting began, what was Quentin's involvement with this film?

Quentin's involvement was very hands-on in the writing of the script. He became involved in writing certain dialogue passages and certain things like that once we got the story down. After that, he was involved in the casting a little bit, but pretty much, he was shooting *Jackie Brown*. And he was shooting that in the summer of 1997, and by the time we went off to shoot our movie, he was already promoting *Jackie Brown*. So I went to South Africa to make this movie and talked to him a couple times about hiring some post-production people. That was about it. I'm sure he was actively involved with Bob Weinstein and Lawrence Bender, but I mostly dealt with Lawrence Bender exclusively. I dealt with Robert Rodriguez, too, early on in the game. He read one of the drafts of the screenplay to make sure everything was cool and to his liking. And Robert was involved with the casting a little bit, too. He really thought Robert Patrick was a great casting choice to appear in the film. So much so that when he saw the dailies on our film, he said, "I'm gonna get him for *The Faculty*."

I understand that you introduced Quentin and Lawrence Bender. Is that right?

Yeah. A friend of mine, Sheldon Lettich, who wrote and directed quite a few Jean-Claude Van Damme films, first introduced me to Quentin. Sheldon and I had co-written a low-budget film called *Thou Shalt Not Kill, Except*, which I also produced. And Quentin was stuffing video boxes for Imperial Entertainment. At that time, Sheldon had a script called *Bloodsport* that was being made into a Jean-Claude Van Damme movie. And Quentin goes, "Hey, man, you co-wrote *Thou Shalt Not Kill* with Scott Spiegel," and blah, blah, blah. "You know all those guys?" And he goes, "Yeah." And then Sheldon calls me and says, "Hey, there's this guy who really knows all his stuff. Would you like to meet with him?" So I said sure. So I met with Quentin, and he gave me his script for *Natural Born Killers* and I read it. I thought it was fantastic. And at that time, I believe I had introduced Quentin very briefly to Lawrence Bender. We were outside the Vagabond Theater and we were gonna meet Vincent Price. We were in line and Lawrence was like, "Hey, I gotta go to this party. I can't wait." But they met briefly.

Then about eight months or so after that, I reintroduced Quentin and Lawrence at a party I was having. And that was pretty much the taking-off point. At that point, Quentin had already finished a script called *Reservoir Dogs*. And Lawrence was just like, "Hey, let's go make this." I think what I tried to do was set Quentin and Lawrence up for *Natural Born Killers*, but Quentin's friend Rand Vossler was already set to produce it for Quentin. And they had that script for several years and nothing was happening. When Lawrence and Quentin hooked up with *Reservoir Dogs*, it just went lightning quick. Boom! Lawrence got Harvey Keitel involved, and obviously the rest is history.

And in the meantime, I hooked Quentin up with a guy named Bill Lustig, who then bought Quentin's script *True Romance* for fifty grand. So all of a sudden, Quentin had money. But really, the key thing I did for Quentin was to set him up with Robert Kurtzman. Bob was looking for a writer to fashion his screenplay from his treatment of a movie called *From Dusk Till Dawn*. So I turned him on to Quentin, he hired Quentin, and that was Quentin's first movie money. You've gotta understand, Quentin was as broke as they come. He didn't have a car or anything, and he'd come out from the South Bay and crash on my couch for the weekend and we'd go hang out and shit. And that was Quentin's first money—$1,500 to write the first draft of *From Dusk Till Dawn*. Then after that, I hooked him up with Bill Lustig, and he sold *True Romance* and got some dough. Then I hooked him up with Lawrence, man, and they never looked back. [Laughs.] Well, they looked back enough to go, "Hey, Scott's cool. Let's get him a movie going."

You and Quentin have been friends for a long time. Have you ever discussed any other collaborations?

Well, we kind of came up with a story for the sequel to a movie called *Relentless* that Bill Lustig did. I was gonna let Quentin run with that. We kind of came up with a story, which ironically Quentin reminded me a few years back, was basically the plot to *In the Line of Fire*. And I'm like, "Quentin, what a memory you have. I don't really, you know. I kind of remember it and you're off one project and you're on another." Bill Lustig used to give me work when I first came out here. I did have an uncredited rewrite on this movie called *Hit List* with Lance Henriksen and Jan Michael Vincent. He'd always throw work my way, polishing up some of the *Maniac Cop* scripts and stuff like that. So I had forgotten that we had that. We kind of kicked around some other stuff, but I was just surprised that Quentin would even be involved story-wise on this sequel because it was not really his top priority. And he was actively involved in the writing of it, which I thought was pretty fucking cool. At this stage, I have no idea. Anything can happen. We're still friends. We still hang out like that, so who the heck knows?

Why didn't Quentin take a screenwriting credit on From Dusk Till Dawn 2*?*

Quentin asked me if he could get a co-story credit while writing *From Dusk Till Dawn 2*, and obviously I agreed. As the credits were finally determined, we discovered Quentin was not and does not intend to be a Writers Guild member. Duane and me are both Writers Guild members, so this posed a problem. But Quentin's name is on the poster and the movie at least three times, which is not counting his company, A Band Apart, which is on the film and poster I don't know how many times. So it's not like we're wanting for his name on the credits. Also, as executive producer, it's kind of part of his role to contribute ideas. It's just that Quentin is a writer/director himself, and so his contributions were perfect. They were just right on the money, so it really made things better.

A lot of critics criticized you for attempting to write Tarantino-like dialogue, when in fact, unbeknownst to them, he actually wrote a lot of that. Does this make you laugh?

You gotta love it. I suppose if Quentin did get co-story credit it would have squelched a lot of those comments.

At the end of the film, Bo Hopkins asks why vampires would rob a bank. To this, Robert Patrick gives him kind of a bullshit answer. Why do the vampires rob a bank?

Because we're talking trailer trash guys who need the money. And, as they become vampires, this does not deter their objective. I'm sure when Vlad the Impaler was first bitten, he needed money, too. You've got to start somewhere. Not every victim is independently wealthy. They've got to buy shit. They can't kill for every little thing they need. As Robert Patrick says, "I suppose vampires need money like anybody else." And these are some relatively low-budget vampires.

You've said that your favorite scene (involving a discussion of anal sex) got cut from the film. Is there any chance we'll ever see a director's cut of the film?

Maybe. *From Dusk Till Dawn 2* is the biggest selling direct-to-video movie in Miramax history, so there's a good chance of it. Also, that direct-to-video label kind of bothers me since the film was theatrically released in fifteen markets with radio promotions and midnight shows. So technically, it's not really direct-to-video.

How would you assess Quentin as a filmmaker?

He's fucking dynamite, man. He's like a triple threat. Writer/director/actor, and maybe quadruple threat.

Quentin was pretty good as an actor in From Dusk Till Dawn.

He really hit pay dirt with *From Dusk Till Dawn.* But the critics still slammed him. I think they will kind of slam him to tell him, "Okay, we really love your writing and directing. Don't act." I think Quentin's really cool. He's taught me a lot in terms of, with him it's all in the dialogue and the characterization, the way he structures his screenplays. I knew it when I read *Natural Born Killers.* I'm like, "Why hasn't this guy gotten this fucking movie made?" I wanted to do it, but it was their baby. He was just like, "How'd you guys do *Evil Dead*? How'd you guys do *Thou Shalt Not Kill*?" He was asking tons of questions and really wanting to know. You see a lot of these film-type people who know everything and then they write a script and you kind of go, "Oh." It's tough. Believe me. It's a really tough game. But with *Natural Born Killers*, after five pages, I was like, "Fuck. This is dynamite."

And his directing style's really kind of dead on and in your face. I love his choices. I love the way he directs a scene.

GUILLERMO DEL TORO

Guillermo Del Toro is, like Quentin Tarantino, one of the most talented screenwriter/directors on the planet. His impressive filmography includes such noteworthy films as *Cronos, Mimic, The Devil's Backbone, Blade II, Hellboy, Pan's Labyrinth, Hellboy II: The Golden Army, Pacific Rim,* and *Crimson Peak*. In addition to these projects, Del Toro has also produced many more prominent box-office films. In 2010, Del Toro, along with cinematographer Guillermo Navarro, established Mirada Studios. The screenwriter/director has received many accolades during his career, and his film *Pan's Labyrinth* was nominated for Best Foreign Language Film by the Academy Awards.

In talking with him for another project, I learned that Del Toro was a huge fan of Quentin Tarantino's work. So, on a Saturday morning in Austin, Texas, we discussed Tarantino's work over eggs and salsa in a small diner called Las Manitas.

You're a fan of Quentin Tarantino's work?

Yes, I am. I am, but in a different way than most people are. I mean, some people like the hip, violent aspect of Quentin, which I particularly don't like. But I like his sense of randomness, which I saw for the first time in *Reservoir Dogs*. I think he is a really good filmmaker in the sense that, for me, each of his films is better than the preceding one. He is progressing. And I think that maybe he's progressing towards the things that his quote unquote "fans" like the least, but I like the most. I think he has a great sense of the accident. How things that are supposed to be glamorous are not glamorous, and are really pretty fucking shabby. And that's what I like. *Reservoir Dogs* had some of that, but *Pulp Fiction* had even more. Like the moment where Vincent is taking a shit, and he left the machine gun on the counter, and the pop tart comes out and Bruce Willis kills him. It's just random. It just happens. Or the guy who comes up with the gun and he shoots time and time again, but he doesn't hit anyone. These are things that in many, many strange ways evoke the randomness of real life. One film that I think does that masterfully is *Jackie Brown*.

Jackie Brown is a criminally underrated film. Why do you think that is?

It's because of the reason I told you. It's like for me, Robert Rodriguez is not going to be fully recognized until he makes a comedy. And yet he's categorized as an action director. I think he's much more of a comedy director, and I think Quentin is a really human director. Most people that are his fans like him because of the hip violence. But he's much more than that. It's a bit like watching Charles Chaplin do *Monsieur Verdoux*, the movie where he plays a killer. People didn't like it back then. They were saying, "This isn't funny. This is not Chaplin." It's filled with funny moments, but people didn't like it. I think people saw *Jackie Brown* and they said, "What is Quentin doing? This is not the usual, you know, crack a joke and blow someone's head off." And I think that was all in credit to Quentin. I think he's constantly evolving, and I personally and subjectively think he's evolving for the better.

It's interesting that he gets this reputation of being so violent, and yet much of the violence in his films takes place off-screen.

That is true. But I do think he uses violence. I think the problem with a work of art like a movie is that it is seen in a very ephemeral context. With contemporary movies, whenever they come out, people have an urge to analyze, classify, and file them immediately. It's like they believe these films need to get their proper place in film history in the first week of opening.

And that is not true. I think that Quentin's films have had an unfair interaction with their audience, meaning we live in violent times. Audiences that have the gangbanger sensibility respond to the violence in Quentin's films in a way that the films themselves are not fully responsible for. I think the films use violence, but they use it sardonically and sarcastically, and they use it almost as a comedic or throw-away element. The violence in Quentin's movies are, for the most part, not real. And then there is the occasional slicing of the ear, which is absolutely uncomfortable. And that's the way that violence is supposed to be. In Quentin's work, the violence is either comedic, which in theory as an art piece should make it almost abstract, or very real, which in theory, should produce a little catharsis in the spectator by feeling completely uncomfortable with violence and stopping thoughts of it. I think the pornography of violence is in the Rambo movies. But I don't think the violence of Quentin's movies engulfs them. I think with time and perspective, they will gain their rightful place in history. But he is, without a doubt in my mind, the single most influential young filmmaker of the end of the century.

Tarantino catches a lot of flak for using homages. As a big film buff yourself, do you think it's the cardinal sin it's made out to be?

No. I think you are the sum of your parts. You either rip-off your life, or you rip-off someone else's life. I think there's no more to art than that. I think the time of true creation is lost in history. What we have had for the past couple of centuries is re-creation. I think if you look at the history of culture you find that culture grows through assimilation. You can see Moorish influences in the architecture of Europe, and there are European influences in the architecture of the East. And from that it grows into a different form. In the medieval times, when countries began importing cultural things and bringing cultural items back from the wars, I think that culture began growing rapidly. When the continents started communicating in the fifteenth and sixteenth centuries, culture grew faster. And I think it has grown faster in the last four centuries than ever before. And in the last twenty-five years than in the last two centuries. So it's exponential. The more you cross-pollinate, the faster you grow culturally. I don't know if it's better or worse, but certainly you evolve faster. And I think Quentin is a part of that. I think Quentin cross-pollinates faster and more eclectically than most people. We can watch a Z-movie and think one scene is great and take it as genuinely as a Venetian architecture traveling to Constantinople and seeing a great Moorish piece of architecture and bringing it back to Venice.

I think more often than not, Quentin dramatically improves upon the scene he's borrowing from.

Of course. And people talk about *City on Fire*, the Ringo Lam movie? I think *Reservoir Dogs* is miles ahead of that movie. I'm sorry. *Alien* ripped off *The Terror from Outer Space*. So? Is *Alien* a better movie? Yes. It is, even though the storyline is one hundred percent the same. I think that sometimes you can steal elements and make them better than the last people who used them. Let me give you an analogy. I think that using elements that come from the media or other movies is absolutely transcended postmodernism, which I hated. Postmodernism was absolutely despicable, but I think in Quentin and the post-Quentin films, it is done lovingly. It is not a reflection so much as it is assimilation. I hated self-reflected movies. I think that movies that reflect about their own genre are very hard to get right. But Quentin is not doing that. Quentin is assimilating a very old tradition and regurgitating it into a totally different form. Quentin takes the film noir tradition and mixes it with seventies' exploitation action flicks and a new form emerges. It's not *The Killing*, and it's not *Foxy Brown*. It's something in between. He's not doing Kubrick, and he's not doing exploitation. He's doing something that is Quentin. It's in between. He melds the influences into his own language.

After Reservoir Dogs *and* Pulp Fiction *came out, a lot of filmmakers ripped off Tarantino's work. For the most part, these films didn't work. Why do you think that is?*

Well, I think with the exception of *2 Days in the Valley*, which

I thought was good, I believe the rest of the films came from insincerity of feeling. You can say anything about Quentin, but no one can say he doesn't sincerely love his movies. He's a guy who gets a boner from watching exploitation films, and that absolutely true love comes across in his work. I think most of these other guys don't really love it, but they think it's hip, so they do it without any passion. Without any real sense of creation. I think fertilization of any work of art needs passion. And those rip-offs are totally devoid of it. Insincere. They are insincere rip-offs and Quentin's films are completely sincere. A man cannot simulate an orgasm. And in that way, a filmmaker cannot simulate sincerity. Frank Capra could have done anything, but I'll bet you he believed in the things he was talking about. I don't know if he applied it to his own life. I don't care. He for sure was a believer in the American dream. Steven Spielberg: you might agree or disagree with him, but he is sincere—especially in his adventure movies. He surely believes that *Indiana Jones and the Temple of Doom* is a great movie. You might or might not like it, but he's as sincere as Kubrick is in shooting *Lolita*.

I know that you have a particular appreciation for Tarantino's masterful casting.

It pisses me off that Quentin is judged only by his contemporary moment, this moment in time in which he is trapped. I think that with a little perspective, people should be able to see that he is a guy who is generally ballsy. When an artist tries something different that is not safe, he should already be awarded with applause for succeeding at it. And that's how Quentin casts. In this way, he's similar to Andy Warhol, the artist. Quentin takes elements that are usually treated with a total lack of respect from other people. I mean, I don't think anyone. . . . Of course, now it's hip to like Sam Fuller now. And that came to be true through '70s film critics that started valuing the anarchist, hip sensibility of Sam Fuller. Very few people would have the balls to say, "I like '70s exploitation movies! I think they're cool." And Quentin came out, made what he did genuinely, and made a powerful act of appropriation. Art is all about appropriation. Him taking

Robert Forrester and making him into a main player, at a point in Quentin's career where he could have gotten Robert Duvall and Alfre Woodard to do the characters Forrester and Pam Grier play in *Jackie Brown*, requires balls and requires a purpose. Quentin has both. He has the balls to say, "I want Pam Grier. I want Robert Forrester." Instead of making the advisable career move and start working with award-winning actors, he has the balls to say, "Fuck that. I want those two." He not only does that, but appropriates them and all of their baggage culturally and transforms them into Quentin actors and into Quentin characters. And that is the same act of appropriation that Warhol would do with the Campbell's Soup can. He would take an object that you would usually not look at for more than two seconds and then enshrining it into a work of art, which is the reason why Warhol succeeded in the pop movement. Because of his concept. And I think Quentin has that loving, caring act of appropriation. He had it in the beginning of his career. Sorry guys, but Harvey Keitel was not exactly a prestige actor at the time he did *Reservoir Dogs*. And he became what Harvey Keitel is again now. He had that '70s period with Martin Scorsese, and he was great. And then he had a lull which lasted almost two full decades. And then he became Harvey Keitel again. As *the man* with *Reservoir Dogs*. Look, a year before that he was making *Monkey Trouble!* So don't fuck with Quentin!

Then Quentin takes John Travolta, who was making talking dog movies. He was, at the time, basically a cheap, has-been actor that you could get cheap for your crappy talking dog movie. And Quentin takes him and makes him into a star again. Those are acts of ballsiness from Quentin that remain genuine because they are done with love. As I was saying, these other filmmakers who make what are called Tarantino-esque movies—if they were given the opportunity to suck dick and cast some star like Tom Cruise in their next movie, they would! Oh, they would just gladly fumble their asses into the studio's hands and cast anyone who is considered bankable. Quentin, right at the peak of his career, chose to go with Pam Grier and Robert Forrester. That is a guy with balls.

BILL UNGER

Bill Unger has witnessed the inner-workings of Hollywood from several perspectives: he has been an agent, a talent manager, and also a television and motion picture producer. During the seven years that he worked as a talent agent, first with the Ufland Agency and then with the short-lived Ufland-Roth-Unger Management Company, Unger worked with such clients as Jonathan Kaplan, Joe Pesci, and Robert De Niro.

In 1993, Unger produced *True Romance*, which was written by Quentin Tarantino and directed by Tony Scott. He has also executive produced Scott's *Crimson Tide*, on which Tarantino did an uncredited rewrite, and *The Fan*. In addition, he is also the president of Tidewater Entertainment. Unger was extremely helpful with this book, and found time over a two-day period for this interview, despite a hectic schedule.

What elements attracted you to True Romance?

I was attracted to the project because of the writing, because the writing was so extraordinary and exciting, in my opinion. The dialogue was brilliant. I read *True Romance* before Quentin began to shoot *Reservoir Dogs*.

When I met Quentin, he was tall, and I'm short—no judgment implied; I'm like five-five, and if you've met Quentin or seen him like the rest of the world now, you know he's a very tall guy. But he was this kind of very tall, very intense, and very much in my face because he knew who I was, guy who asked me if I had read any of his screenplays because he had sent them to me. And this was actually at a party at Tony Scott's house. I was talking to Shane Black, whom I knew, and Quentin kind of came across the room and was introduced to me by a woman who had once worked for me and was currently working for Tony Scott as his assistant. And he just started talking, and I was fascinated, you know, but had no sense of his talents as a writer. I remember telling him I hadn't read his screenplays. I was even aware they had been sent to me, but I told him I would look at them. He was kind of dazzling, but without the history and the credentials, frankly. He was also very eccentric, and I didn't know if he was the real thing or not.

I located his screenplays. Actually, the first one I located was *Reservoir Dogs*. I gave it to the person who was working with me at the time doing coverage, and asked him to read it and tell me what he thought. The person gave it really bad coverage, which I understand is pretty much what had been happening to Quentin with his submissions of *True Romance* around town. And, based on the coverage, I hadn't read anything. Then I heard shortly thereafter that he was in fact going to do the movie because Harvey Keitel had become involved. I actually had been in an acting class with Harvey in New York years before. I knew Harvey and I knew he was very serious about his work. He had a very serious taste. So I thought, maybe I'd better read this. So I picked up *Reservoir Dogs* and I got no further than four or five pages—the now famous opening sequence—and recognized how special it was. Right there, I stopped and called Quentin up on the phone and said, "Let's have lunch. Let's get together right away." And we did. We got together the next day.

I had finished the screenplay by then and was no less impressed than I had been with the first four or five pages. I was just really excited. I told him so, and he was very sweet, very flattered, very respectful and complimentary. It took me a good part of the lunch to get him to stop calling me *Mister Unger*. I told him I thought he was a very special talent and asked him what else he'd done. He then asked me if I had read *True Romance*, and I confessed that I hadn't. I'd forgotten that he'd sent that as well. He said, "Well, that screenplay's really available. I wrote that first, and I would love for you to read it because I'm a big fan of

Tony Scott. I would really love for Tony Scott or you to be involved and I think you might like it a lot. I think it's available." That's how he put it to me.

I promised that I'd read it that night, and I did. I was really excited, and I called him. He then told me to call his agent at William Morris. It took me two or three weeks to get a return call. That spoke more about the agent at that time than my status in the business, because I got return calls from heads of studios. I told Quentin and he was really frustrated, but again Quentin was quite unknown at the time. I finally got someone else at the agency to call me back, who told me I should speak with an attorney who represented a French man who had optioned the rights to *True Romance*. His name was Samuel Hadida, whom I'd never heard of, and was talking about doing it as a low-budget action or exploitation movie. And Quentin hadn't really mentioned any of that to me. I then put in a call to the attorney, who then told me that Samuel Hadida was coming to town. That began the dance with *True Romance*. I called Tony Scott and told him that he should read it because I thought it was very exciting writing and it had great parts for actors and that it was something he would really respond to. That kind of began the whole thing that took quite some time before we got it done.

One other thing to tell you that was really remarkable that I remember about Quentin is that we had a lot of lunches after that first meeting. He then invited me to the set of *Reservoir Dogs*. He was shooting in the Valley, so I said I'd come over after he was into shooting a while. He said, "No, no, no. Don't wait. Come over as soon as we get started. I'd love to see you and stay in touch. I want you to meet everybody," and he was again very inviting. One of the things that struck me, because I'd been involved with and had associations with an awful lot of directors, including a lot of first-time directors who really went on to gain a lot of recognition, was how self-confident he was. And it wasn't a swagger. It was almost like there wasn't any question of why he wouldn't be able to do what he believed. I was very impressed with that.

I waited until day two of shooting, despite the invitation, and did go over. And there he was. It was about a hundred degrees in this garage in the Valley. He introduced me to Lawrence Bender, whom I had never met before and who really had no idea what was going on. Not in any negative way do I mean that of Lawrence, but again, it was basically day one for him, too. He was beginning to realize he had a bit of a tiger by the tail, I think. But Quentin. . . . When I came on the set, he stopped what he was doing. He was gracious, he was cordial, he was focused, he was attentive and no way distracted by what his responsibilities were. He was genuinely enjoying himself, and I again was very taken with that. The people around that seemed to be really picking up on that. When the lunch break was over, he immediately and very easily went back to what he was doing. He apologized for going back and again, the stress, he seemed to thrive on it. I took note of that as well.

I called Tony Scott again and I said, "I think this is a very special guy." Tony said he had read *True Romance*. He said that he loved it and asked what I thought about us doing it. I said I would explore that because the rights were more complicated that Quentin had given me reason to believe. That was kind of the beginning of it.

Some critics called True Romance *a senselessly-violent film. Do you think that's a fair assessment?*

I think it is an unfair assessment because I don't think it is a senselessly-violent film. I think it is a violent film, but I think there was a great deal of sense behind that violence. I think that, in fact, I myself had real concerns about the making of the movie. While we were making it, there was a lot of thought given before we decided to do it. Tony Scott and I had a lot of very serious conversations about it during post-production and during a two week, really moment-to-moment discussion with the ratings board. It was very much present once we began shooting and while we were shooting. Of course, *Reservoir Dogs* had been completed and had been distributed and had received an awful lot of both notoriety and acclaim. I think the issue of violence is really kind of something Quentin has since become identified in some ways. This was all very conscious to us. And I think violence is a part of the story and the characters and the culture that this movie is representing. I think that there are moments in the movie where it's arguable that that shot or that moment or that scene—do you need it or not? I could, quite frankly, argue it either way. There was, amongst the people involved in the movie, and I'm including Tony and myself, very passionate disagreements over some scenes and some specifics. But I think in the end, the movie is what it is and is what Quentin intended it to be. I think it's a movie that people should be very aware of, before they see it, that it's violent and that it's not for everyone.

While I was making that movie, I did not allow my kids to see one piece of it, and they didn't attend the premiere and they were very frustrated because I made the judgment that they were too young for it and that it was not appropriate for them. But now they're grown, and I would not restrict them from seeing it. Interestingly or not, they still haven't seen it.

Really?

No, but they know Quentin and they know that work, but they're teenagers now and it's a different matter. So, I think it's violent. I don't think it's senselessly violent. That's the short answer.

How different was the screenplay from what ended up in the final film?

That's a good question. There are so many changes that take place, even when it's a single-voice like a writer/director. When it's a screenplay that is in existence and a director comes in, there are always changes depending upon casting, and locations, and budget, bright new ideas and bushy-tailed new egos, all kinds of things. I can tell you that essentially it is absolutely the screenplay that we began with, with two key differences that I'm certain of. One is in Quentin's original, as I read it and recall, everyone in the room at the end is killed. Certainly the lead didn't survive. I'm trying to remember how he dealt with how the story was told. I also think an answer to that is the opening voiceover narration and ending voiceover narration were not part of the original ending. Those were mostly the work of Roger Avary.

Quentin was unavailable and uninterested at the time of changing the screenplay, so we asked Roger to help. Roger and Quentin discussed it, and Quentin said, "You can do it if you want to. There's no one I'd rather have do it." So, during pre-production and a little bit during post, some of that work was done. Quentin did come in at the end. What we did was we described the problem and he wrote it out quickly. The voiceover that ends the movie is mostly his. The fact that the young lovers survived wasn't part of Quentin's initial scenario and that is the major change.

There is very little, amounting to almost nothing, that I can remember that's different. Not in terms of voice or structure, and not really even in terms of dialogue. The other thing to keep in mind is that Quentin at one point called me and said, "I'm heartbroken. I hear you're going to shoot the ending as Hadida had wanted it." That had been one of the things that had been troubling Quentin about Hadida's vision—a slightly different vision where the lovers survived. Quentin said, "I know these people. I know what happens, and they don't get out of that room." And there was a discussion that it would be shot so it could be edited both ways. Quentin was concerned that it was a commercial consideration specifically. Tony Scott's point of view was that it was wrong. He wanted them to survive. He had fallen in love with the characters, and he wanted the audience to fall in love with those characters. "I don't want them to die at the end. I want them to survive." Tony felt very strongly about that, and Quentin came to accept it as another point of view—a valid point of view that was simply different from his own. As I understood it, he very much came to accept that.

Those are basically the changes I recall.

How much of what was filmed of the cunnilingus discussion scene with Samuel L. Jackson does not appear in the director's cut?

Well, there are two key things that aren't in either cut. I think that scene is problematic partly because it was shot early in production and also that scene was kind of the first day we had Gary Oldman. You know, we had Gary coming in and out, and we had Chris [Slater] coming in and out, and we had Val [Kilmer] coming in and out, and we had Brad [Pitt] coming in and out. It led to a very interesting kind of rhythm to the production. What I think happened, as I always understood the scene, was there was this joking going on amongst the gangsters, and the younger guy was getting picked on because of his attitude toward cunnilingus. They riffed on him. But as the scene ends. we see that Oldman and his sidekick are playing the young kid and Jackson for fall guys. They were just setting this up. Though it builds up the tension in the scene, I think the humor is lost a little bit in the beginning. That was always my point of view. And Gary had hurt himself on a stunt very early on, and it was a little difficult.

In terms of the dialogue, what I had an argument with Tony was, there was a line that Jackson's character had that was Quentin's line. He turns to the young brother, and when he is angry and getting picked on by Oldman's character, he says, "You white guys screwed it up for us." And Jackson turns to him and says, "You don't get it. It's not a race thing. It's a taste thing." And it was such a shocking and funny line. It was also a line that, when included in a couple of the earlier cuts when we screened it, I felt immediately relieved an awful lot of the tension that I felt was in the audience concerning Quentin's language and particularly the way he deals with race. People just did not know how to act, and it created a lot of tension. And that line in relation to what is going on with the audience. . . . That line, I think, is such a great line in that, to me, it always basically says the truth—that sex is more important than race. Stop it. That's not what we're talking about here. And he does it in such a frank and surprisingly street way that you could just feel the audience kind of exhale and use that as kind of permission to move on. But for some reason, Tony didn't think the line played, so it got dropped.

In terms of the way the rest of the dialogue was in that scene, there was no ad-libbing as I recall. There was no improvising and none of that was rewritten, so it's essentially played as is. And there's no real difference between the director's cut and the release cut except that we had this murderous battle with the ratings board with the man who headed the board for years. He took offense to the number of times the word pussy was used. And so, as I recall, we literally had memos going back and forth amongst grown men that we were laughing at, but almost crying about, too, that in the first cut the word pussy is used twelve times and now it's limited to seven times. We would then get back a memo that it wasn't enough. So would be looking at each other and kind of asking with a sense of absurdity how many times you could use the word pussy and not offend this man. What that scene's about is being outrageous, so there's not a difference between the release cut and the director's cut in terms of content. It's just that the dialogue riffs a little longer and there are more references to cunnilingus.

That scene began the battle with the ratings board, which ended with the end and most difficult part. That was the scene with Patricia [Arquette], where she breaks free and kills the assassin. And again, there was something about that scene that was very important to all of us that the ratings board objected to and that we had to change.

You were the executive producer of Crimson Tide, *which Quentin did some uncredited rewrites on. Tell me a little bit about why he was called in and what some of his contributions to the script were.*

Well, I don't think that story's really known, and it's been mis-told, as far as I'm concerned, every time I've heard it told. It's kind of hard to tell it brief because it's complicated and it is amazing in many ways much more than any other association I've had with Quentin.

From my point of view, in regards to what happened and what kind of difference he made, at the time, Tony Scott did not have a film to direct and was kind of having a difficult time making up his mind as to what he was going to do next. I heard there was a screenplay at Disney called *Crimson Tide* that Hollywood Pictures was going to green-light and give a quick go to. There were political reasons for that because they were in trouble and the head of the studio at that time was clearly in trouble and he wanted to green-light a picture and make it work. So it was going to happen very fast. It was not developed by [Don] Simpson and [Jerry] Bruckheimer. It was developed by the studio. An executive at the studio with the writer, and the basic structure of the story was worked out by them through a number of drafts. They handed it in and it was then given to Simpson and Bruckheimer, who had not really done anything since they'd been at the studio, so they were looking for something as well. It was a group of people that had had real success in the past that Tony Scott was very familiar with, as was I. For a good action movie, it made sense and was creative. So I got a call, and they said, "If you guys want to do this, you'll have creative control."

Jerry Bruckheimer called and played it Jerry Bruckheimer-cool. He said, "Well, what do you think?" When I read the screenplay, I said that I thought the story was absolutely terrific because it had two characters in a very dramatic and legitimate conflict. What I liked was that you could easily argue either case. You didn't have to have a bad guy, and that's something that is exciting to me. I also told him that I'd been raised in a Naval town and that I knew what it was like to stand on a hill and see a huge and powerful ship decorated and going out to sea. No matter what your politics or your feeling, there's something amazingly exciting about that. Inspiring, I guess. That feeling was contained very much within the screenplay. I read it. I liked it and I called the studio and told them that, and they asked what Tony thought. I told them he hadn't read it yet, but that I was going to give it to him. I did, and he read it, and he didn't like it. I asked him to look at it again, and he said, "I just don't respond to it. I don't know if I want to go back and work that way with that team again, either."

The truth is that I was looking for someone to help me persuade Tony that my point of view made sense. Quentin was my friend, and he was someone that I knew and was very much respected by Tony. I called Quentin, who was in the editing room on *Pulp Fiction*. I called and said, "Quentin, I need your help. I've got a screenplay, and I think it's very good potentially. It's got problems, but Tony doesn't understand why I like it. I'd like for you to read it and tell me whether you think I'm crazy or not." And, to my surprise, he said, "I'll gladly do it. Send it over to the editing room." I did, and that night, very late, around one o'clock, I got a call from Quentin, and he was very excited. He said, "I know why you like this." And we started to talk about the screenplay and the characters and what could be done. Then he said, "I think I know where some of the problems lie. I think I know what things work and what things Tony probably has issues with. If you'd like, I'll do the rewrite for you." I never expected that. He was in post-production and was well, well, well on his way to being the public Quentin Tarantino. I just didn't think he'd have the time or the interest.

And he said, "You know, I think this is a cool movie and I'd love to be able to do a big rewrite," but he said it on some terms and I had to remind him later. He said, "I don't want credit for a variety of reasons," including the Writers Guild, and I think also because he wasn't sure how much work he'd be able to do and when he'd be able to do it. He also said the screenplay in terms of story really worked out pretty good and he didn't want to diminish the credit of the writer. Another reason, I think, is because he was very sensitive about the way the public touted Quentin as a darling of the independent world and Tony Scott was so often critically dismissed by the independent world. Quentin is a genuine and huge fan of Tony Scott, and when *True Romance* came out, I think he felt that there was kind of a free-for-all about "What's good is Quentin's and what's bad is Tony Scott's." I think he was sensitive to that as well at that particular moment. So I said, "Look, let me call Tony, tell him, and speak to the studio. When the heck would you do this?" I told him it was only a few months away, and he said, "Well, I'll be able to do it right after I do my cut. It shouldn't take me more than a couple of weeks." So I called Tony, and he was, as I would have expected, thrilled. He trusted Quentin so much so that he said, "If Quentin commits to doing the rewrite, then I'll commit to direct it. We'll all do it together."

And [Jeffrey] Katzenberg, who was an early studio fan of Quentin's, was over the moon, as were Bruckheimer and Simpson because they really wanted Tony to commit. So we all made a deal, and the deal—Tony's involvement, my involvement—was all contingent on Quentin doing the rewrite. Then we were given a casting list of seven people, and we started to meet with leads. We worked out everybody's deal, which took quite some time. And during this time, the rewrite couldn't proceed, because that's what people were focusing on—the production issues, as well as the casting issues. Quentin was editing, and there was really very little and no discussion of what was going to happen on the rewrite. Also, Quentin had asked that he be left alone. He said, "I don't want studio notes. I don't want director's notes." He said, "Here's what I want to do if it makes sense to you—I'll talk to you and I'll deliver it." And everyone accepted those terms, although they were unusual and a little disquieting. It took so long for a variety of reasons after a number of different episodes that Quentin went off to Cannes while pay-or-play deals were made with Denzel Washington and Gene Hackman. He went to Cannes and he of course won the festival, and he still hadn't done his rewrite. Meanwhile, we were inching towards principle photography, and people were in a panic because they were waiting for him to do the work.

The work was, frankly, that he was going to give greater dimension to the characters. In the first draft we read, the Gene Hackman character was called "The Bear" and the Denzel Washington character was called Hunter, and all of the other characters had very little dimension. And there was no humor at all and the dialogue was different, except for the dialogue that involved the instructions and Naval commands. Tony was very concerned, the studio was very concerned, and all of us as producers were very concerned. During this time, I was the only one that was in touch with Quentin. He was traveling and he wouldn't give out his number to anyone else. He insisted on that. I couldn't get him often. He just kept saying, "I'll do it, I'll do it, but I'm not sure when I can do it."

Then he called me up well beyond the last minute and said, "You know, Bill, I can't do it. My heart's not in it. I can't find the voice. Everyone was to kind of tell me what they wanted me to do. Then I needed to know who was cast and then you didn't cast for awhile." He was feeling tremendous pressure from this big movie and all of these people, and I think he didn't want to do it. So I said, "Okay, this is what I would call a legitimate disaster. I don't know how, but I'll deal with it. Quentin, you can't do what you can't do or won't do, and this was all because this was going to be good for all of us. You weren't supposed to be abused and/or suffer if you were going to do this. This started out of a real generous act of friendship. "I was thunderstruck because I think the sky would have fallen on many heads. I think mine would have been the one that would have received the most debris. When I said it was okay, he said, "You know, don't say anything. Let me think about it a little more." I said I was going to sleep, and he said, "I'll call you."

He called back (and I didn't wake up) about four hours later, probably five or six in the morning L.A. Time. He left a long message, and he said, "I've been walking around and I've finally got the voice of the captain." Then, off the top of his head on my answering machine, he basically gave Gene Hackman's speech when he gathers the troops before they board the submarine. He says, "Little ducks, there's trouble in Russia, and they've called on us." It was just this wonderful, inspiring kind of speech, and he gave the whole thing. He said, "Bill, I can do it. I'm gonna do it. Don't say anything to anybody. I'll be back and I'll talk to you." He came back four or five days later. I told everybody to hang in. He asked me to hire him a secretary, and he locked himself in a hotel room and he kept doing the rewrites. He'd call me every once in a while to read something. The whole scene with great momentum concerning the mutiny—the dialogue between Denzel and Gene. He wrote all of that. The initial interrogation of Denzel, the setting up of that.

The truth of the matter is the story didn't change. The story is almost identically what it was, but qualitatively and significantly there was a great dialogue change.

So Quentin, as is usually reported, being brought in to provide a few X-generation jokes, is obviously as I just told you *not* the story. He brought an awful lot to that screenplay, which reads very well in the drama and the conflict of the two men. And the actors loved what he wrote, by and large.

RAND VOSSLER

Like most of Quentin Tarantino's friends during the Video Archives days, Rand Vossler dreamed of working in the film industry. So, when Tarantino and Craig Hamann embarked upon their amateur film *My Best Friend's Birthday*, Vossler volunteered to help. Working many hours and receiving no pay, Vossler served as co-cinematographer and producer on the film. After that, he produced a music video for Pearla Battala's "Dance Me to the Edge of Love," which starred Tarantino as a young groom. Later, Vossler was attached to direct Tarantino's screenplay *Natural Born Killers*, but was ultimately removed when producers Don Murphy and Jane Hamsher were unable to secure funding for the film with an inexperienced director at the helm. After Oliver Stone entered the picture and took the reins, Vossler served as co-producer on *Natural Born Killers*.

How did you first meet Quentin Tarantino?

Basically Quentin and I met through my brother Russ, who at that time worked at Video Archives during the whole "Archives crowd days." Quentin wanted to do a short Super-8 film called *My Best Friend's Birthday*, and Russ really encouraged him to get ahold of me because I'd been taking film classes. I had worked on probably thirty small films at that time; you know, 60mm student films and such. And he set up a meeting at Quentin's mother's house in Torrance, and we sat down and met each other through *My Best Friend's Birthday*. At the time, the screenplay was about forty-one pages. Quentin had dreams of doing it on Super-8 with some other friends of his—Scott McGill, who worked at Archives at that time, and Craig Hamann, whom Quentin knew through the James Best Theater Group. And we basically got together and read through the screenplay.

I loved Quentin's energy, and we just chatted each other up, and I decided with much enthusiasm to encourage him to scrap the idea of Super-8 film and to lengthen the screenplay into feature-length form and shoot it as a 16mm feature outlaw. *Stranger Than Paradise* and *She's Gotta Have It* were two of such films that had come out directly prior to that. And Quentin and I jumped on that right away. We were speaking the same language and basically started making the film together.

You served as cinematographer for at least part of My Best Friend's Birthday. *Is that right?*

Yeah, for the majority. Actually Scott McGill, who was a closer friend of Quentin's, had done probably four or five Super-8 films and actually had a great, great eye. I've said this before, but at that time, he was probably the most talented of all of us so far as having a distinct style. As a filmmaker, he just did everything himself: chopped the films, cut the films, scored the film's music, and just had a great sense of narrative that was just lacking in most of the student films I was working on at that time. He was supposed to be the cinematographer, and I came onboard *My Best Friend's Birthday* after all of the basic plans had been laid and they had already done some casting on the film. The idea was that I would sort of help out and be a liaison for getting equipment and helping to set things up. Very quickly, Quentin and I became partners creatively and Quentin, never having shot anything, didn't know anything about camera work and setting up the shots. Basically, with Quentin, everything [at that time] was just from being a film fan but not necessarily knowing how things worked.

But Scott McGill was the cinematographer for the first three or four days and I was assisting him. We basically would set up the big shots, and just so far as energy and pace, we needed to be working at about twice the clip we were working on. And it became pretty apparent, at least energy-wise, that something needed to change. Scott kind of stepped down and said, "Rand, you know what you're doing here. You should be shooting this film and I'll assist you." He basically became my assistant and I took over. Scott had never shot 16mm film and was kind of intimidated by the process, not that it's really much different at all.

What's your assessment of the sixty-five minutes or so of My Best Friend's Birthday *that was completed?*

Actually, there's quite a bit more footage than sixty-five minutes running time. So far as the quality of the film, we were told many times by numerous people that so far as the style of photography and the quality of performances, it was some of the best 16mm footage that many people had ever seen, which motivated us greatly to get the film done.

Have you heard anything in the press or in any of the books about Tarantino that you knew to be incorrect? Sometimes it's difficult to distinguish between what's true and what's legend.

Well, here's what I've learned about the press and the media, which is a constant fascination of mine and will continue to be so—there are stories out there that kind of get built upon and built upon. Then a lot of them have been dispelled as joking stuff, like when Quentin and I were working on putting together *Natural Born Killers*, we kind of created these personas for ourselves as filmmaker guys. We wrote bios for ourselves that weren't true to be more legitimate, and a lot of those little things get picked up on. You know, somebody says something that was based on partial fantasy. Obviously, the domino effect has become these big stories. One of them, as I'm sure you've heard, was about Quentin being in [Jean-Luc] Godard's *King Lear*. Stuff like that, that is basically blatant fabrication, but its genesis started from little stories. We figured no one was ever going to see Godard's *King Lear*. It was, "We'll just say that Quentin was in that," and all of a sudden he's got instant validity and some credibility. There was a very short phase where that was something that we both felt we kind of needed to push ourselves. Then Quentin becomes this huge superstar, and somebody finds an old résumé or an old bio of his and says, "Hey! Quentin's in *King Lear*!"

What's great is that he continued to support that story for quite a while. He admits that it's obviously a lie, but he said something to Jay Leno like, "As far as I'm concerned, I am *in* King Lear.*"*

Oh, exactly! I mean, that's the whole thing. With Quentin, he's really become a master of manipulating the media. He understands the media and he understands that it's a tool, and so far as he's concerned, Quentin definitely knew how to be a success. He knew what it was gonna take and what he needed to do.

At one point you were attached to direct Natural Born Killers. *How did you become involved with the project?*

Quentin and I kind of had a falling out when he started to cut *My Best Friend's Birthday*. In hindsight, he really kind of looks at that era as his film school days, having never been to film school. Basically, the first time you shoot film and try to cut it, you learn more than you will for the rest of your career in that first project. I think at one point he kind of made the decision to scrap *My Best Friend's Birthday* and direct his energies towards a new screenplay, which was *True Romance*. And I think the idea was that he'd get Roger [Avary] to put it together and to produce it for him, and basically Roger would take my role—what I was to *My Best Friend's Birthday*. So he took that on and was trying to get it packaged with Roger. I actually hadn't spoken with Quentin and we'd had a little bit of a falling out.

I went on and started working in film shortly after *My Best Friend's Birthday*, and kind of left Quentin to do whatever he needed to do with the project. He and Roger got involved with two English producers, Stanley Margolis and Peter Thompson, and basically went into development hell. They tried to get that project done through raising money, and Quentin was eventually asked to step down as director, which he did begrudgingly. Based on his stepping down and Roger's supporting that step down, he basically said, "Fuck those guys." He then went to hammer out the first draft of *Natural Born Killers*. The first version of that was written in late '89, and it was just this outrageous road film with Mickey and Mallory as the stars. Wayne Gayle was, I think, barely mentioned in the screenplay within the *American Maniacs* sequence. He was not a character unto himself; he was just basically a background guy. Quentin called me out of the blue saying, "Rand, I've put this new screenplay together and blah, blah, blah, this is what happened with *True Romance*, and how would you feel about doing the film ala *My Best Friend's Birthday*, guerilla style? You know, shoot it however we can get it done, working on weekends, whatever." I had an office at the time at MGM, working with Lewis Chesler and doing development with him on some cable shows. Chesler had just started getting some things together to do some feature development in the range of $2 million films with French and Canadian co-producing. And I was like, "Quentin, goddamn, bring this thing by and let's get it together and see what it is!"

He sent me a copy of it, which I read immediately, and he and I got together at Denny's. We sat down for the first time in a while, and the first hour of our discussion was just talking about *My Best Friend's Birthday* and what that experience was. And I knew going into that that if we were going to work together again, we needed to kind of iron out what the working situation was going to be so that a) the film got done, and b) we both had a sense of what we were going to be doing for each other. We began ironing out the responsibilities and apologizing for the distance that we had prior to that.

Natural Born Killers was, at that time, this bold, outrageous road film that was so distinctly written for the purpose of shock and had all the extremes that Quentin knew he had to put in the material so that basically nobody else in the world would want to direct it but him. He was protecting his material. Coming off *True Romance*, where he was asked to step down, it was a pretty bitter pill for him to swallow, and he was determined to write a screenplay and he would just immediately turn that money around and we would start shooting *Natural Born Killers*.

He and I began working together immediately again and took

over my office at MGM and actually pitched the idea to Lewis in hopes to raise some money. And again, as with everything, once Quentin and I got together with material, we immediately talked each other up about how grand it would be if we could do this with it, and this with it, and this with it. In addition to the material evolving, we were also trying to think about how much money we could raise to get the film made. It was, "Is this something we should be doing for thirty grand or $500,000? Or a million? Or two million?" We immediately began putting together partnership packages for independent financing. We then pitched it to Lewis, who showed it to another development person, who didn't get it, so Lewis didn't pull the trigger on getting us developed. So I basically quit my job in development in order to pursue working with Quentin in the development of *Natural Born Killers*, and was able to keep my office there. We worked out of MGM and out of an office on the Sony lot, which was actually prior to it being Sony. We just worked nonstop, month after month, trying to raise the money.

During that time, Scott Spiegel, a friend of Quentin's, had just sold his screenplay for *The Rookie*. He'd made like a half a million dollar sale on the screenplay, or something like that. Scott Spiegel was now hot shit around town, and was getting a bunch of work thrown his way for rewrites. He then passed a lot of that work on towards Quentin, who would do these little rewrites for Cinetel and other companies. That was kind of like that whole era where Quentin was doing this little work and we were meeting at my office everyday to do everything we could to raise money for *Natural Born Killers*, with me as the producer and Quentin as the director. We put together a whole production package for that. That's when we generated all the biographies that we sent out with all of those packages. We actually raised a pretty decent chunk of money along the way. Where the whole me coming into this as the director came from was basically a reaction to *Reservoir Dogs* getting picked up.

How did the infamous Hun Brothers scene come about?

I was introduced to this guy as a possible avenue for independent money. And this is still early *Natural Born Killers*, still trying to raise the money independently by pitching to doctors, dentists, lawyers. It was make the money at all costs. We were kind of turned onto this guy who lived in Manhattan Beach and drove the fancy car and talked the whole talk. He'd never been involved with film before, but he had these two guys he kind of represented. I have no idea where this guy made his money or what his whole deal was, but he had these two seven-foot-tall Nordic twin bodybuilder behemoths who really wanted to get into the movies. Basically, after meeting upon meeting, we finally got to sit down and meet these guys. They really wanted a part in the movie, and they were willing to give us somewhere around $120,000 to put them in it. Our whole goal at that time was to raise $500,000 and then take that money and do a matching funds kind of deal so we'd have a million dollars to do the film.

We had worked out several budgets. We had a million dollar budget and a two million dollar budget and so on and so forth. We were prepared to do it at any point with however much we raised. The whole deal was that we put together a sequence. We didn't want to give these guys real substantial roles in the film because we had no idea what their talents were, and what can you really do in a film with two identical seven-foot Nordic bodybuilders? What kind of film are you gonna make with *them*? These guys were huge. At the time, I thought that Quentin had written the scene. I later found out that Roger had written it for the film because Quentin was disgusted with the idea of writing a scene for money.

Anyway, it was a three or four-page scene about the Hun Brothers, which was a direct parody of the Barbarian Brothers, who ended up playing the parts in Oliver's film. Basically, the two brothers are movie stars, and they just happened to be the latest victims of Mickey and Mallory. I guess during the course of their attack, they recognize the actors and they're like, "Hey, you guys are the Hun Brothers! I love your films!" It was a great scene. I love that scene. It was so hilarious. I mean, here you have these two guys who have been mutilated and have had their legs chainsawed off, but they're delivering this really intelligent interview with Wayne Gayle that's just filled with all this admiration for Mickey and Mallory.

Were there any aspects of Stone's rewrite that you really liked or disliked?

Choices that Stone made that I really can't stand are making Mickey and Mallory white trash, which defeats what those characters really are. It's the whole thought of serial killers being the guy next door, the girl next door. Once you regionalize those characters, you're doing them a great disservice. To me, Mickey and Mallory have to be the ultimate icon of the Ted Bundy, the really good-looking movie star. Everything about them really should have been that. They should have been the Elvis Presley and Ann Margret of the '90s. They should be these icons of Americana, so I think he really sabotaged the characters by making them so kind of white trash-y and Southern drawl-y. That's one thing that I can't stand about it.

One of the scenes I thought was brilliant was the *I Love Mallory* sequence, which really doesn't have a place in that film. But it's a great idea, and so far as selling his view, it goes a long way. It's an absurd, abstract, surreal sequence that does speak within the theme of what we were trying to say with the film. I just thought it was a brilliant scene, but it really doesn't belong in the film. The whole notion of Wayne Gayle and attaching all that stuff to the media was to keep the relationship with the audience and how they perceived Mickey and Mallory versus who Mickey and Mallory really were.

The idea was to keep that as a constant back and forth. We would kind of give the audience a bone to like them and then take it away from them. If you look at the structure of our final draft and think about it as kind of this progressive humanizing and dehumanizing of characters, you will see that this is a theme we were working for. It's a theme I kept pressing on Quentin to continue working on and to mature that. It really has a brilliant arc if you look at the way that [the original screenplay] was structured. The opening scene is a bunch of rednecks with Mickey and Mallory in a roadside truck stop. You've got rednecks who, in film language, are expendable. You've got Mickey and Mallory, who are obviously the stars of the film, who are so good-looking and so cool and they've got the leather jackets and the leather pants. You've got the foxy chick who's dancing the dance and the cool-headed guy who is sittin' back, and they're animals who are ready to strike at any moment. And you've got a redneck who's trying to pick up on the woman. And right there, those are the ingredients for some kind of violent act, which we accept as a movie-going audience. And of course, we're not let down. There is a good reason that the violence in that scene is way over the top. It's hyper-violent. It's like the ultimate expression of movie violence taken to the next step. Just outrageous, non-plausible, operatic bloodletting. That's the way we wanted to open the film.

Directly after that, you have the '50s splash titles with a Duane Eddy tune playing. It's just like you're set up for an outrageous movie experience right off the bat. The next time you see Mickey and Mallory kill is a little bit later in the Wayne Gayle sequence, and they're killing a cop. And killing a cop, in movie terms, is cool. It's black and white. You have bad guys and bad guys kill cops. We already know that's what happens in these kinds of movies. We as an audience accept that. I don't think anybody lost sympathy for Bonnie and Clyde when Faye Dunaway turns and shoots a cop in the face. Thus, we still root for Mickey and Mallory as we do with Bonnie and Clyde in the sense that we disconnect ourselves from the reality of what these people are doing because we're enjoying them so much. We're enjoying them, and they're sympathetic characters. In the screenplay, the third time we see them kill is in the scene when they go wipe out the family, which just happens. You're just thrown in there, and they're walking through a middle-American suburban home, going from room to room and graphically slaying this family, which meant to be everybody's family. It's meant to be your family. And it's at that point when we want the audience to all of a sudden rear up and say, "Hey, this was fun before. That coffee house scene was fun before. Mickey and Mallory kicking the ass of rednecks was fun. This isn't fun." There's no way to justify Mickey and Mallory's actions at this point. That's the end of the first act, and that's really where we wanted the audience to realize that Mickey and Mallory really aren't cool. And it's then that we introduce Jack Scagnetti. It's then that we introduce the warden.

It's then that we introduce these as kind of like the main characters of the film now. It's no longer a film about Mickey and Mallory. Those guys were built up as icons in the first few scenes of the film, and they are continued to be related to as icons through the Wayne Gayle stuff.

Then Mickey and Mallory are captured and they go to prison and they are dehumanized. It's then that we start getting to know these characters that we recognize are worse than them. I don't mean worse than them to the extent that Oliver Stone really took both the Scagnetti character and the McClusky character and turned them into outrageous stereotypes. They were never meant to be that. They were always meant to be these people who are in it for themselves. They're all trying to manipulate the situation to their own end. McClusky's got this plan to hire "super cop" Scagnetti, who had just written a book on his last big case, to get them out to the desert and basically manufacture some accident that kills Mickey and Mallory, because a cult following has started around them and the warden sees this as a bad thing. They're not human to him, and he wants to wipe them out. So all of a sudden, you get the separated lover thing, and Wayne Gayle is introduced. He's this flag-waving potential spokesman for Mickey and Mallory, and he's really only in it for himself. Scagnetti's looking for a Pulitzer Prize. Wayne Gayle's looking for the Edward R. Murrow Award. And you've got McClusky, who just wants to wash his hands of these two.

Mickey and Mallory are the only true characters. It's like you have to respect the shark. The shark swims and eats, and that's a very simple way to look at Mickey and Mallory. They are what they are. Within this film, there really are no characters that you can like. If you don't like what Mickey and Mallory are doing, you can't be along with them, and that's cool. But you've gotta respect those characters because they're the only honest characters within the structure of the film. That was really the whole point of it.

Another scene in Stone's version that I couldn't stand was when Mallory goes out and seduces the guy at the gas station. Those are things that just would not happen with Mickey and Mallory. These two live for each other. There's a constant connectiveness with them, and the notion of sexuality outside that expression with each other would not and should not exist with those characters. They live for each other and are in the truest sense a partnership. And it's sold that way in the film. If you look at all the stuff and all the dialogue with Wayne Gayle, there's an operatic love. And all of this stuff that's sold in the film as the way the American public responds to Mickey and Mallory is basically the way we should, as a film audience, look at and respect the notion of what the essence is of these two characters. They would be classical mythological romantic figures if they just didn't kill people. If that happened, all of the Romeos and Juliets would pale by comparison in the sense of connection that these two characters have. That's what Wayne Gayle sold to the American public within the structure of the film, and that's what everybody responds to. That's why they get the big cult following. That's why they are the superstars that they are. Obviously, the point with making the film was to hold a mirror up to the face of the audience and to say, "Okay, if you don't like these characters, why do you watch Donahue and Geraldo, and now Jerry Springer? Why do you tune in?" Where is the problem? Is the problem with the Mickeys and Mallorys? No. I don't think so. As an artist, I don't think so. I don't think that's the problem. I think we all have a fascination with what yellow journalism and sensationalism is all about. That sells. We want candy.

Quentin and I knew that people would talk about this film. Come hell or high water, people would hate it, people would be appalled by it, people would leave the theater, but they would talk about it.

That reaction was evident with the release of Stone's film. There seems to be no middle ground. It's a film that people either love or hate with no room for anything else in between.

Oh, absolutely! And that was the intent with the project. Quentin and I always said that you've got to make a splash with your first film. This is the type of film that would do that. *Natural Born Killers* should have been Quentin's first film. I mean, he made plenty of splash with *Reservoir Dogs*, but I would have loved to see Quentin do *Natural Born Killers*. I would have loved to see that film! Not to badmouth Oliver Stone, because I think he's exceptionally talented, but he has a talent of soap boxing with his films, and he'll get the biggest soap box and the biggest mallet and go to town. How much of the subtlety of *Natural Born Killers* is wasted because you get beat over the head with it?

I think Oliver Stone is a great filmmaker. I love Platoon *and* Wall Street. *I even like* The Hand, *but subtle is something that Stone is definitely not.*

Absolutely. You know, people laugh when I tell them that *Natural Born Killers* was supposed to be a very subtle film and that was the concept from the get-go. Not subtle in the violence. The violence has got to hurt. You've got to feel that pain when Mickey and Mallory wipe out that family. It has got to be the most difficult scene to watch in the history of cinema. You've got to feel those gunshots; you've got to feel those knife stabs. You've got to feel that pain and you have to be put through that whole experience. The whole arc of loving these two characters and then hating them—you know, one-third of the way through the film, and then taking the next two acts and having the audacity to try and rebuild those characters in the eyes of the audience was the glory of that screenplay. And that's lost completely. That's not there in the Stone version. Obviously he either didn't get it or he had more important things to say, or he had things to say more frequently that we did. I would love to one day sit down with Oliver Stone and have a conversation with him regarding this film.

Had you and Tarantino made Natural Born Killers, *how might the film have been different?*

This is like a real tricky thing because after Quentin left *Natural Born Killers* and went on to *Reservoir Dogs*, I did copious storyboards and copious notes. What Oliver Stone did with it visually so far as the color theme, so far as his aggressiveness with the cut, with the editing, so far as his aggressiveness with the visual styles, all that Indian shaman stuff—I'd get rid of all that shit. That doesn't belong there. That's sort of like post-*Doors* Stone that he just stuck in there. Obviously, that stuff has no place in that film. There's nothing mystic about Mickey and Mallory. They are who they are, and the whole idea of introducing some kind of mystic element to that film is just Oliver Stone masturbating.

So far as what the film would have been. . . . Again, I think it would have been a slightly different project if Quentin had directed it first and me produce it for him versus me directing it and Quentin being gone directing *Reservoir Dogs*.

Okay, let's drop Tarantino from the equation for just a moment. He's working on Reservoir Dogs *and you're directing it. How is it different?*

Different from Stone's version?

Yeah.

It would have really respected the fact that Wayne Gayle was the true lead character of the film and that Mickey and Mallory represented, through the film, icons, and that they really do need to remain that at the end of the film. A lot of it has to do with what we were talking about before in the subtlety and arcs of the characters.

We have Mickey and Mallory being these hyper-icons of Americana. We get them halfway through the film and you're dehumanizing them, basically rebuilding them up through the connections we have with the media. You know, we all turn on the tube. When the next big car chase that O.J. is in happens, you'd better believe that every fucking television in the nation's going to be on. People are going to be watching that because that's what the public eats. That's really what needed to be said in that film that didn't get said. It's talked about, but it's not really felt by the audience. There's really no connection to the audience's responsibility in what that film is trying to say. That's what's missing from the Stone version is that it really gets caught up on. . . .

You know, I can really see Oliver Stone sitting around saying,

"Wow! This is really super cool! Let's get five or six writers, and let's sit here and brainstorm about other cool scenes!" And that's where you get shit like the *I Love Mallory* sequence. It's totally playing on the theme of the film, but it just has no place in the film. It's kind of pieced together. Ironically, that's kind of how Quentin writes! [Laughs.] That's one of the big ironies of it. When Quentin sits down to write something, he doesn't map things out. He writes. He just sits down and he writes a scene. And it's a great scene and it speaks for itself and has arcs within it and characters that you love to hang out with. Then Quentin sits it aside for three years, and then when it comes time for him to write his next screenplay, he pulls out all of his notes and says, "Oh, this is a cool scene. Oh, this is a cool scene." And then, all of a sudden, he's got the structure of his new film. That's the way a lot of his stuff came about. He would just write a scene and he'd watch a movie and say, "God, I love this scene in that film, but I can do it better." Then he'd sit down and fire off a scene. One of the scenes in the first draft of *Natural Born Killers* was a scene where Mickey and Mallory were holed up in this roadside gas station, and there's like some dippy gas jockey who's there and they kind of have him held hostage, but he's harmless, so they don't have him tied up, and the cops are surrounding the place. And they start taking pot shots trying to kill Mickey and Mallory and there are bullet holes with light streaming through. And the whole genesis was that Quentin saw some crappy Emilio Estevez movie. And that was Quentin saying that he loved that particular scene and that he would do it and do it better. It's the borrowing of a concept and applying it to something completely different. That's how *City on Fire* or *A Better Tomorrow* gets stuck into his films.

MATT WAGNER

Pennsylvania-bred comic book writer and illustrator Matt Wagner started his career with a story that introduced the world to the assassin character Grendel. That character would ultimately become the stuff of legend, resulting in not just its own title but two Grendel/Batman crossovers. Perhaps best known for *Mage*, Wagner has also worked on many established characters, including the villain Two-Face for the graphic novel *Faces*. Wagner is also responsible for Trinity, a series combining the forces of Superman, Batman, and Wonder Woman. In recent years, he has been closely associated with Dynamite Entertainment's *Zorro*, in which he reimagined the classic character from the old West.

This led to the Wagner-written crossover comic *Django/Zorro*, which served as an official sequel story to Quentin Tarantino's film *Django Unchained*. Speaking on the crossover, Tarantino told reporters, "I loved the idea. One of the things I liked so much, I grew up reading Western comics and entertainment in general, whether it was the Zorro comics, or the Disney show, or *Zorro's Fighting Legend*. What I thought was such a great idea was taking the most famous fictional Mexican Western hero, and putting him together with one of the most famous black Western heroes."

Were you a fan of the original film Django Unchained?

Oh, fuck yeah. I had a friend who's a local reviewer take me to a press screening. He told me later, "I've got to take you to more of those." Because all the critics sit there very seriously considering the film, and I was just laughing and howling and clapping. [Laughs.] I just enjoyed the hell out of it. I'm a fan of Quentin's stuff in general.

How did you become involved with the Django/Zorro *comic?*

The whole project was put together by Nick Barrucci, the guy who runs Dyamite. He was a long-time friend of Reginald Hudlin, who was a producer on Quentin Tarantino's film. They just kind of put this idea together, I think half-joking to begin with. Then things started to get more serious, and Nick contacted me and said, "We're talking about doing this. Would you be interested in writing it?" I just thought, *That's never going to happen*, but I said, "Sure. If the opportunity comes up, I'd love to do it, but it's not going to happen." So I completely forgot about it, and then four or five months later, I got another very energized call from Nick. He says, "I sent Quentin all your *Zorro* stuff and he loves it. He wants you to come down next week to talk about this." Even then I was like, *really, no, it's not going to happen*. But then, yeah, it all came true. I was surprised, but they pulled it off.

What was meeting Quentin like?

Here again, I was like, *This could fall apart at any minute*. Quentin's such a famous guy, and I'm sure there are about a million people demanding his time. Even when I pulled up to his house I was thinking, *Something's gonna fall through*. [Laughs.] But no, he met me at the door. He pulled me in and took me and showed me his comics right away. He has a very unique and cool box where he keeps his comics. If we're not the exact same age, Quentin and I are pretty close in age, so our cultural touch points are kind of similar. His is, of course, more movie oriented, and mine more comic oriented. But I know plenty of movies and he knows plenty of comics.

Did you guys talk a lot about other comics?

Yeah. He had just gotten back from this big San Diego con,

and he had bought up a whole bunch of the oversized black-and-white magazines that Marvel used to publish in the '70s. That just thrilled the hell out of me, because I had loved those when I was young. Even though they didn't have very strong subject matter in them, they felt more adult when I was buying them at twelve and thirteen years old. I guess because they weren't racked with the other comics—they were racked at the magazine rack. So he had maybe fifty or a hundred of those, and we just pored through those and reminisced.

I read that Quentin was adamant that Zorro be the same Zorro you had already redefined at Dynamite.

When I went down there, I was thinking we're gonna have to have a legacy Zorro, since *Django* occurs so much later than the Zorro adventures. But when we first started talking about it, he was adamant: "I want the old Zorro." Considering Django's relationship with King Shultz in the film, where he already had this openness towards having an older mentor-like character, it just fit like a glove. Then we had to talk about what had happened to Django since the film, because this took place about two years after the film. He told me Django's wife was down in Philadelphia, and that he'd taken her there. He was very much a wanted man. It had taken them a long time to get out of the South. They had fought their way out of there, and Brunhilda was now working with the Underground Railroad. So he's gone back to doing the only thing he knows how to do, which is bounty hunting. And he just keeps pushing farther and farther West because there's not as much institutionalized racism out there.

Did you get much direct input from Tarantino while working on the project?

Sure. We spent two days with the first go-around. I had already heard this from somebody else, but when Quentin first starts working with you, he likes to screen movies for you. So he had a whole litany of stuff he wanted us to watch in this very cool, very comfortable screening room. So we watched a couple of films, and we watched a couple of chapters of old Zorro serials. We'd kind of watch a little bit and then go up to his porch and chat, working out storyline stuff. So when I went there to meet him, I was down there for two days. It was a very open, very free-form kind of meeting. I didn't know if I'd need to come back the second day. We didn't even know if we'd get along. But he said, "No, no, no, you've got to come back tomorrow so we can keep working on this." I went back to the hotel that night, and I wrote the first six pages of the script to kick it off and get it started, so I could get direct feedback from him in regards to Django's voice in particular. One thing he cautioned me about, he said, "Don't try to write black dialect. Try to write more cowboy dialect." Of course a few of Django's enunciations are more black than cowboy, but that was a very cool and insightful bit of direction.

So then I came back and started to work on it, and maybe three months later I contacted him and said, "We need one more meeting. We've got the general outline, but now that I'm kind of blocking it out, I have a few more questions for you." So I went back down for another afternoon, and we got everything accomplished that we wanted to do. He had very quick answers for each of my questions. And it was valuable, because there's a scene in there that's a flashback where Django remembers a little adventure with King. That scene was actually in Quentin's first draft of *Django Unchained*. He still had it in handwritten form. But he'd cut the scene because he felt it was a little repetitive and that the film was already long enough. He brought this up because I felt we needed some sort of reminiscence about King, because he was such a powerful figure. With this being the first new Django adventure, I thought we needed to see King in some fashion. He had the scene already, and we found a place where it fit in nicely. He pretty much acted the entire scene out, telling me all of it. He kept telling me he was gonna get me his original handwritten script, but he never did because he got started on *The Hateful Eight* preproduction. And when you start working on a movie, boom, you just disappear into that hole. Since he had acted it all out for me, I just kind of wrote it from memory and just filled in the spots that needed filled myself. I was pretty happy with it. I felt that I hit King's voice pretty well.

How much freedom did you have in crafting this story? Did you ever feel at all hamstrung, having to answer back to Quentin?

No, he was really open to everything. Again, he really loved my version of *Zorro*, so when I went down the second time, the questions I had were very specific. I said, "In all your films, there's some chunk of pop culture." In *Django*, you could argue that that's not there, but it is. Mandingo fighting was a pop culture thing of its time. You could almost compare it to the S&M dungeon in *Pulp Fiction*. We were determined to examine racism not through black people, but through the local indigenous population. I said, "We need something the Indians do that signifies their despair. A dark, sort of subcultural thing." So he very quickly came up with the idea of playing chicken with sticks of dynamite. That fit right in and certainly fit the bill for what we were going for. The other big thing was when I told him we needed a significant death of some kind. So I suggested we kill Bernardo, Zorro's longtime servant and brother-in-arms. And he just thought that was a terrific idea.

What are some of the challenges you faced on this particular project?

The big challenge was that it wasn't as neat a pairing as I had originally thought it would be. I had thought, yeah, that sounds neat. That sounds cool. But the two characters are very different ages, and they come from very different worlds. That's always fun to meld, but one operates completely incognito and the other one doesn't. So I found in writing it, I really couldn't have the two of them fighting back to back, so to speak, until the grand finale. Otherwise, you've got one guy in a mask and another guy not in a mask. The bad guys are gonna go, "We don't know who that guy is, but go get the other guy who doesn't have the mask on." [Laughs.] They're also very different in their approaches. Certainly in the heat of battle, Zorro will kill somebody if he has to. But he's not like Django, who will just happily blow their head off. It was a really neat challenge trying to make those work, and I think I pulled it off.

What are some of the challenges to writing for someone else's character as opposed to one you've created yourself?

Both of those are somebody else's character. Over the years I've done a lot of that. I don't know how familiar you are with the comics industry, but I'm sort of more known for my two indie characters, Grendel and Mage. Over the years I've had lots of opportunities to work with other characters for other comic companies. I've done lots of Batman for DC. I've done lots of stuff for Dynamite, like *Zorro, The Green Hornet, The Shadow*—all those old cool pulp characters. I'm currently working on the relaunch of the Will Eisner character The Spirit. I find it an interesting challenge to play with someone else's toys like that. One difference is that with a character like Batman, you have a history of like seventy-five, eighty-five years. You're kind of free to pick out the stuff you like and toss out the stuff you don't. But with something like The Spirit or with Django, you're suddenly working with a character that is closely identified with one particular voice and one particular author. So that's a neat challenge also—to try and strike that author's tone, and yet bring something of your own to the table, as well. Ever since the death of Ian Fleming, you've seen many officially-sanctioned other people writing James Bond books. And some of them are more successful than others in striking that tone.

What are some of the joys and challenges that came with writing about an older Don Diego character?

Once Quentin suggested that to me, it all sort of made sense. He also brought up another interesting factor in that Don Diego sort of puts on this foppish demeanor to deflect people from his true identity and adventures as Zorro. Quentin pointed out that after that many of years of living like that, wouldn't he actually become that persona? Wouldn't he actually be that kind of fussy, older aristocrat? And I thought, *Yes, he absolutely would.*

Quentin hints at the beginning of issue one about a possible future Django/Lone Ranger team-up. Is that something we might actually see?

They haven't contacted me, so I don't know. I don't write *The Lone Ranger*. If they did that, I would think they would turn to one of the regular Lone Ranger authors. I don't know. Maybe. I wouldn't say no.

What kind of feedback did you get from Quentin once the comic was finished?

He loved it. I would say for the first half of production I heard from him pretty regularly. Then, again, he started *Hateful Eight*, and I didn't hear from him until the end. I would assume with that he's keeping watch over me with his character, and I'm sure that once he saw that I could handle it he was okay with it. He told me at the end he loved the way it turned out.

What elements of the Django/Zorro *comic are you the most proud of?*

Meshing these two characters that, on my second thought of it, didn't seem to mesh as well as I initially thought they would. I'm certainly proud of having had the chance to work with Quentin. He's really one of the most vital film directors working today. I've enjoyed his work for many, many years. Also, my son colored the book, which was pretty cool. I think it just turned out beautifully.

DUANE WHITAKER

Pulp Fiction may not have made Duane Whitaker a household name like it did for Samuel L. Jackson, but it is surely the role with which he will most frequently be associated for the rest of his career. Whitaker played Maynard, the rapist pawn shop owner who takes Butch and Marsellus hostage.

In addition, Whitaker wrote and starred in *Eddie Presley*, which Quentin Tarantino appears in. Along with Boaz Yakin and Scott Spiegel, he also co-wrote the screenplay for the Tarantino-produced *From Dusk Till Dawn 2: Texas Blood Money*, also appearing as one of the robbers in the film.

Other notable Whitaker appearances include the films *Tales from the Hood*, *Feast*, and *The Devil's Rejects*.

You first met Quentin Tarantino while filming Eddie Presley. *What was your first impression of him?*

I was pretty surprised. He's actually pretty calm and normal. We just got into a conversation. Basically, we'd both worked with Lawrence Tierney. [Laughs.] So that was all we talked about. He was sort of a common enemy. I think maybe I had met Quentin a couple of times in passing prior to that.

Had you already seen Reservoir Dogs *at that time?*

No. It wasn't out yet. At the time when we were doing these pick-up flashback sequences, I don't think the film had been released yet. They had sold it and it had done festivals or whatever it had done where it caused all the stink, but I don't think it was physically out yet. It was pretty close. I mean, it was right around that time. But I hadn't seen it.

The film Eddie Presley *disappeared for almost seven years. What happened to the film during that period?*

There were a lot of different reasons [why it disappeared]. It played some festivals and never really got a good deal. They never got a good offer on it. It just sort of floated around and it was really spread out. I mean, some of the people involved with it lived in Texas, the investors, you know, and some live out here in California. It was kind of a nasty scene there for awhile. Finally they agreed—everyone agreed—to just get it out there. But it actually played on the Sundance Channel for about a year-and-a-half there a couple years ago. So that was really the first time it was out there. A lot of people saw it then.

I understand that most of Quentin's scene was cut out of the film.

It was sort of a cameo thing. I'll tell you what it was supposed to be: it was supposed to be Quentin and Sam Raimi, playing these attendants at this nut house where my character's been locked up. And Sam got a better offer, I think. [Laughs.] So Bruce Campbell stood in for him. At the last minute it became Bruce and Quentin. It was just one little exchange, and somehow along the way, most of it got cut. You know, I certainly didn't do any of that! [Laughs again.] It was maybe two or three lines apiece. It was supposed to be a little cameo thing, but it became even less than that. But Quentin was at least on screen.

How did you become involved with Pulp Fiction?

This is actually kind of amusing. I was working. I'd just done a couple of films, writing screenplays and getting these little acting jobs. This is actually a true story, as weird as it sounds. I actually ran into him at a coffee shop in Hollywood at about three o'clock in the morning. He was by himself and I was on my way out. I recognized him and we started talking. "What are you doing?" You know, and I told him what I'd been up to. And he said, "You know what I'm doing?" And I looked completely different at the time. I'd been doing the Elvis impersonator and at this point; I had the hair and the beard sort of puffed out and shit. He sort of looked at me and said, "You know, I'm doing a film. It's pretty much cast, but there's a part that you're kind of right for. I'll have casting call you." I went, "Yeah, yeah, whatever." And it was *Pulp Fiction*. It was almost that stupid. I mean, there was a long process between there and actually doing it, but that was how it started. I just happened to run into him.

That's interesting.

Yeah, it's a very bizarre little thing. [Laughs.] I mean, he was like, "We're gonna call you," and I was like, "Yeah, whatever." And they did call and I did go in and eventually, you know, that's what happened.

What did you think of the character Maynard the first time you read the screenplay?

I thought it was great. I thought it was incredibly clever. I read it and I thought, *Oh, that's really interesting.* I'm reading the scene and the guy picks up the phone and I was just like, *Yeah, that's interesting. He's gonna call the cops.* And then he just takes that ridiculously weird stance, you know. I thought it was just great writing. I thought the whole script was the best script I'd read in years. You know, I'm a writer, too. And I was just totally blown away by this thing. I knew it was gonna be something, but I didn't know it was gonna. . . .

Make the splash that it did.

Nobody did. But I knew it was the best script I'd read in a long time. It was just a question of whether or not it all worked. When you read a lot of that stuff on the page, you're like, *God, this is great, I just don't know if it'll work.*

Do people come to you on the street and say, "Hey, you're the guy who raped Ving Rhames"?

[Laughs.] More than you can even imagine! Yeah. If I go out without my glasses on, it happens. Something about that movie comes up at least once a week. It's a very weird thing, yeah.

What was your reaction to Pulp Fiction's *being named to the American Film Institute's Top 100 Films list?*

You know, I just agreed. Time will tell, but I thought so too. I thought it was a good choice. It's way down the line, though. Where's it at? It's like eighty-something.

But it looks pretty damn good on your resume, being in a Top 100 film.

Oh yeah! I should put that AFI thing on there. [Laughs.] No, I agree. I think it's an incredibly cool film, you know? Time will tell. We'll see if it's still listed on there in twenty years. But yeah, I certainly would have put the film on that list, for sure.

How did you become involved with From Dusk Till Dawn 2: Texas Blood Money?

There was a film that I had written—I wasn't involved in it because I was doing another project at the time called *Tales from the Hood*—and I'd sold the script to Roger Corman. It was called *Zipper's Clown Palace.* They ended up changing the title of it to *Stripteaser.* It's a low-budget picture they did over at Concord that a friend of mine directed. And the director of that film sent it over to Quentin because he wanted him to look at it. I guess for one reason or another Quentin was looking through a bunch of low-budget/no-budget films to see what people were doing. And obviously he knew me, and I think he really enjoyed the movie. It's a very talky movie. It's sort of weird. It's just a strange little movie about a psycho that takes a strip bar hostage. It was real dialogue-heavy, sort of like some of the stuff Quentin's written. I just think they liked it. They'd just set up a deal with Scott

Spiegel to do *From Dusk Till Dawn 2*, and they were in the beginning stages of that. I think he looked at the movie and thought it would be a good idea to bring me in to work on the script with Scott. And Scott and I knew each other. We were at least acquainted. We'd crossed paths a few times. I didn't really know him well, but at least Quentin knew we didn't hate each other . . . at that point, anyway. [Laughs.] So he asked Scott, and Scott said that would be cool. What he told me is that he took the film and showed it to Bob Weinstein and said, "Why don't we hook him up with Scott? He's really good with dialogue and character stuff." I was like the Quentin figure to Scott's Robert Rodriguez figure, you know what I mean? So that's kind of how it started. Quentin called me and asked if I'd like to do it, and I said, "Sure!" Then, several months later, they called me back. They had put the deal together and everything, so we got started on it. But it was all sort of based on that Corman film.

How much of the script would you say you wrote, and what are some of the scenes you contributed?

I wrote the whole script! Scott and I were together through the whole thing. There are a few stories. I don't know where that came from, that I came in and kind of punched it up or something. No, we wrote it from the very beginning together. It's not even as clean cut as I did all the character stuff and he did all the plot. We both did both things. We kind of had a really basic story idea that we started with—that sort of cowboy, *Reservoir Dogs* thing. It was not really plot specific at that point. I mean, we literally sat down and watched a bunch of crime movies and vampire movies and started out pretty much from scratch. So how much did I personally write? Fifty percent.

Do you ever talk to Quentin anymore?

Every once in a while. It doesn't happen that often. We used to cross paths much more frequently. I haven't seen him in a while.

Have you had any lengthy conversations with him?

I've had a few.

He's kind of notorious for his movie arguments. Have you ever gotten into an argument about films with him?

Not really, no. We had sort of this thing about *Poltergeist* that we were talking about once. That whole Tobe Hooper/Steven Spielberg thing about who actually directed the movie. But that's about it. No arguments. Usually whenever we've had long conversations, it's been about business deals.

MIKE WHITE

To fans of Quentin Tarantino, Detroit filmmaker Mike White is about as close a thing to the boogeyman as there can be in the whole Tarantino saga. In 1994, the young filmmaker exposed a number of similarities between Tarantino's directorial debut *Reservoir Dogs* and *City on Fire*, a Hong Kong actioner directed by Ringo Lam, in his low-budget documentary *Who Do You Think You're Fooling?*

To most Tarantino fans, Mike White, who also serves as editor and publisher of the long-running magazine *Cashiers du Cinemart*, is widely known as the guy who "hates Quentin Tarantino." His *Pulp Fiction*-based follow-up *You're Still Not Fooling Anybody* did little to dispel this misconception. In 2013, White broke the story that film writer (and, interestingly, then-Tarantino girlfriend) Lianne "Spiderbaby" MacDougall was plagiarizing existing works in her film critiques.

White is also an accomplished author, having penned the books *Impossibly Funky: A Cashiers du Cinemart Collection*, *Cinema Detours*, and *Mad Movies with the L.A. Connection*. He also served as an uncredited co-writer on cult filmmaker Greydon Clark's book *On the Cheap: My Life in Low-Budget Filmmaking*.

I understand that you were initially a fan of Reservoir Dogs. *What happened to change all that?*

I was initially a fan of *Reservoir Dogs*, and I still am. The caveat comes in my perception of the originality of the film and its director, Quentin Tarantino.

It all started back in the fall of 1993. I had become friends with Mike Thompson in my Film/Video 300 class at U of M [The University of Michigan]. Ironically, though it was our senior year, neither of us had had the opportunity to use a camera during our years of film school. I knew Mike from previous classes, but it wasn't until Film/Video 300 that we actually had a conversation. It turned out that both of us were big fans of Quentin Tarantino's *Reservoir Dogs*. Sure, most of our fellow film students were enamored by that film as well, but none were so vociferous about it as we. One fateful day, however, Mike Thompson dropped a bomb on me. It was something that I could never recover from. It turned out that our hero was not all that he appeared to be.

Certainly we knew that Tarantino was as big of a film geek as the two of us, and that his freshman film was heavily-steeped in film history, especially *noir* tradition. We spent hours talking about where Tarantino got ideas and who influenced his work, as Tarantino didn't seem to hesitate in shooting off his mouth about this film or that in magazine and newspaper articles. We tracked down every video and hungrily watched them, determined to find out what made this wunderkind tick. Mike found out and passed the information along to me, something that he surely regrets today.

Empire, a British movie magazine, broke the story. In a sidebar by Jeff Dawson, the horrible truth was laid out in black-and-white for all the world to see, but for no one to pay attention to: "Quentin Tarantino has been hailed as the hip new messiah of filmmaking. How strange, then, that the basic premise of his legendary movie bears a remarkable resemblance to that of Ringo Lam's 1989 Hong Kong movie *City on Fire*. . . ." Dawson then went on to give scene-by-scene descriptions of actions in Lam's *City on Fire* that were repeated in Tarantino's *Reservoir Dogs*.

I was in shock! How could this be? I became obsessed. How could my hero, the Horatio Alger of video store clerks, be a plagiarist? Say it ain't so!

I looked in the computer system at Blockbuster Video, but found only *City on Fire* by Alan Rakoff. Luckily, John Woo was coming into his American heyday for film geeks and fanboys, and a local paper, *Orbit*, had a great article about Woo and where *gweilo* could find his films. It took a little driving and a lot of patience, but I found Lam's *City on Fire* at the Evergreen Supply Store after going through their hundreds of tapes, video by video.

What I saw shocked and amazed me. Most of the similarities between the two films came from *City on Fire*'s third act—the jewelry store robbery and its aftermath. However, when one puts *Reservoir Dogs* into a linear narrative, it seems that Tarantino's film could not function without Lam's original material.

My jaw still agape, I waited. I was going to be patient about it. I didn't want to pass judgment over Quentin before I had all the facts. Perhaps this information was in the press pack, common knowledge to film reviewers. Perhaps a statement was going to be issued. Perhaps Quentin was planning a press conference to apologize for this oversight. I was waiting for answers to all questions. I waited for the next *Entertainment Weekly*, my Bible. It had never let me down before, always providing me with the most up-to-date information about movies, video, and music. But, the formerly-infallible *EW* let me down. But it wasn't just them. The media was strangely mute. It wasn't that Tarantino had lost popularity and no longer appeared in magazines; quite the opposite. However, while reporters were fawning over him, no one asked the question I wanted to hear: What's the story with *City on Fire*?

I decided that it was up to me to spread the word. I showed those final previous twenty minutes to all of my housemates, who through my temerity all loved *Reservoir Dogs*. Some were angry, some were indifferent, and some couldn't grasp the idea. I realized that I needed a better format with which to make my case. I had waited six months for the media to respond before giving up my hope and taking a few hours at the University of Michigan's shoddy video editing suites to make a full-motion montage showing the similarities between *Reservoir Dogs* and *City on Fire*.

Things were quiet for a while. I didn't really know what to do with my tape other than show it to friends. It never dawned on me to send it anywhere until, months later, when *Film Threat* finally ran a story on the rampant similarities between *Reservoir*

Dogs and *City on Fire*. In order to show them that they weren't the only people who knew of the scandal, I sent them a copy of my tape. For my troubles, I got a call from Chris Gore, the editor-in-chief. Gore was ranting the first time I talked to him about how great my tape was. We talked a few weeks later, and he wanted me to send him the master copy. Since I wasn't pleased with the original VHS editing job (thanks to the crappy gear at U of M), I promptly put my buddy Eric to work, helping me to do it on ¾" tape. We worked long into the night, making a much more acceptable version for Gore to use on the *Film Threat Video Guide's* free subscription video.

A lot of people argue that all artists steal to some degree, be it painters or filmmakers. Early Tarantino collaborator Rand Vossler recently told me that "imitation is the genesis of art." What is your take on this theory in regards to the appropriations from City on Fire?

Not to be rude, but I'd have said to Rand Vossler, "blah, blah, blah." I hear that lame excuse all the time. I usually hear it more as, "good artists paint while great artists steal." Bullshit. Certainly, no one lives in a vacuum and all art is a product of our creativity and influences, but the nihilistic attitude that "there is nothing new" is not only defeatist, but too goddamn glib. Milton would say that since *City on Fire* was "made better by the borrower" that no theft has occurred. And then there are some that say if you don't give credit to your sources in your bibliography then you'll be thrown out of school on your ear. Looking at all of the articles and interviews that Tarantino has done, I'd say that he was given ample opportunity to mention Lam's films.

Before finally admitting that he was a huge fan of City on Fire *and, in fact, had a poster from the film hanging in his house, Tarantino was quoted on MTV news as saying that he "couldn't wait to see the Hong Kong original." Would you have been more sympathetic had he admitted the film's "influence" right up front?*

For the record, that MTV story had far more things wrong about it than right. For one thing, my video, *Who Do You Think*

You're Fooling, had only been pulled from the press screening. During the actual [Chicago Underground Film] Festival, it was shown during three screenings. For another, Quentin's poster revelation had occurred *before* he was quoted as saying he wanted to see the original film.

As for his admittance of using material from *City on Fire*—it never happened. When questioned about the "similarities" between the films, he merely stated that he loved *City on Fire* and had the poster for it, not that he was in any way influenced by Lam's work.

Like I said earlier, the problem came for me in that in magazine and newspaper articles, Quentin was always going on about some film or another, and even did a few Top 10 lists for magazines like *Details* and *Vox*, but never recommended *City on Fire*. Seems odd, doesn't it? When asked point blank by a *Film Threat* reporter, Quentin says *City on Fire* is one of his favorites, but neglects to recommend it. Plus, he never lists it among his influences. Instead, he would simply go along with the journalists' theories about his being influenced by Godard or Melville.

If Quentin had talked about *City on Fire* in those early days, then I don't think *Who Do You Think You're Fooling* would have been made. The only real bone I have to pick with the guy is his silence on the subject. I've often said that if I had known *Reservoir Dogs* recycled elements from *City on Fire*, I might have been even *more* impressed with Tarantino's work. To take large elements from a lousy film and use them so inventively is remarkable. But, to skirt the issue and never completely admit to the impact of Lam's film is inexcusable.

As you may or may not know, Ringo Lam himself completely ripped off Peter Weir's Witness *in a 1988 film called* Wild Search. *How do you think this affects the argument of Lam being a "victim of theft" in regards to* Reservoir Dogs?

What can I say? Two wrongs don't make a right? I don't know if Lam ever *felt* victimized. I tried to arrange an interview with Lam years ago, but was diverted by his American manager. I wonder, though, if Lam made any bones about *Wild Search's* connection to *Witness*. Maybe he's got a *Witness* poster hanging in his living room!

You openly admit that Reservoir Dogs *is a much better film than* City on Fire. *Despite all of the outside things that went on with it, do you still enjoy watching* Reservoir Dogs?

City on Fire is, by no means, a good movie. In the years since my initial viewing, I've only managed to stomach the whole thing once. In fact, I've watched several other Lam films only to be equally disappointed by his tendency to build up major action scenes and then cop out on the payoff every time. The beauty of *Reservoir Dogs* is that the Mexican standoff between Nice Guy Eddie, Joe Cabot, and Mr. White is not interrupted, as it is in City on Fire. The only watchable qualities about *City on Fire* are the performances by Danny Lee and Chow Yun Fat.

I may not watch *Reservoir Dogs* as much as I used to, but I don't think I could keep up the pace of seeing it three or four times a week. I'll still pop it into my DVD player every once in a while, always enjoy a good quote from it, and still contend that it's the best of all Tarantino *oeuvre*. In fact, I regret that *Pulp Fiction* is more popular than *Reservoir Dogs* as *Reservoir Dogs* is a vastly superior film, in my humble but deadly-accurate opinion.

Have you ever met Tarantino or received any messages from his office?

No, I've never met Quentin. I don't imagine he gets to Detroit very often. I've never received any messages from his office, though my phone number and address are readily available to him. I've sent every issue of my 'zine, *Cashiers du Cinemart*, to his Band Apart offices. I talked to his publicist, Bumble Ward, once and was informed that Quentin was "flattered" by my film, but something tells me that she wouldn't tell me if he was pissed about it.

In 1997, you made a companion piece to Who Do You Think You're Fooling *called* You're Still Not Fooling Anybody. *This time, your focus was on a number of much smaller homages found in* Pulp

Fiction. *What made you decide to fashion a second film based on Tarantino's work?*

I've gotten quite a bit of flack about making *You're Still Not Fooling Anybody*. It's been called unnecessary and excessive, and I'm just about the last person who will disagree with that. I made *You're Still Not Fooling Anybody* as a lark. It came after I read, heard, and experienced a series of scenes from other films that were reused in *Pulp Fiction*. Whereas *Who Do You Think You're Fooling* is a narrative documentary, this was just a jokey follow-up.

A lot of reason for making *You're Still Not Fooling Anybody* is that I was bored. It had been a while since I had done a video project, and I wanted to see if what I envisioned—my process of "Plagiarvision"—was possible. Luckily, I had a very technically-adept coworker in my corner, the same guy who helped me in my final version of *Who Do You Think You're Fooling*. I'd talk more about him, but he's always told me that he prefers to be the Roger Avary to my Tarantino. He threatens to talk very badly about me and take credit for everything we've done together someday. [Laughs.]

After having made both Fooling *films and having written some similar pieces in* Cashiers du Cinemart, *you now have a website called "The Anti-Tarantino Site." Some people would label you as being "the Guy Who Hates Quentin Tarantino." Do you think this is a fair description, and do you think this Tarantino thing has become an obsession for you?*

I've always been interested in Tarantino, ever since he burst on the set with *Reservoir Dogs*. Perhaps it's turned into a bit of an obsession, but a healthy one. I'm always curious as to what he's up to, and just how far the extent of his outrageousness might go—I don't mean the plagiarism either—all of his fisticuffs have proven pretty amusing as well! [Chuckles.]

If people take the time to read the material on my website, they'll see that I don't hate Tarantino or his work. You've got to admit that a site labeled "Anti-Tarantino" is going to cause a bit of intrigue and get a few more hits than "Ruminations on Quentin Tarantino and his Propensity to Plagiarize." "Anti-Tarantino" is my attempt to market the site. It pushes people's buttons—one of my favorite pastimes!

What are some other misconceptions that people have about Mike White?

I suppose the greatest misconception is that I hate Quentin Tarantino. I certainly don't admire his acting abilities—though he played a psychotic rather well in *From Dusk Till Dawn*—but I don't hate the man either. He's never done anything to me, except disappoint me by not giving credit where credit is due.

INDEX

2 Days in the Valley 136
21 Grams 33
2000 AD 49

The A-Team 51
Aaron, Jason 49
Albernathy, Ben 46
Alien 136
Alfred Hitchcock Presents 37
American International Pictures 25
American Film Institute 75
The American Folk Theatre 33
Anderson, T.P. 49
The Apple 20
Arquette, Patricia 146
As the World Turns 33
Assault on Precinct 13 87
Avary, Roger 10, 20, 57, 58, 61, 67, 77, 91, 112, 143-4, 157, 185

Bad Dreams 77
Bad Lieutenant 33
Badlands 121
Barbie 84
Barncat Publishing 21
Barkin, Ellen 25
Batman 51

Battle for Ono 103
Beals, Jennifer 33
BearManor Media 20
The Beatles 6
Bender, Lawrence 12, 34, 85, 128
Benji 19
Bernard, Jami 19, 21-4
Bierce, Ambrose 106
Bishop, Joey 25, 27
Bishop, Larry 25-32
Black, Shane 140
Blade 2 133
The Blair Witch Project 16
Blow Out 94
Blues for Minnie 49
Body Double 94
Body Heat 78
Boogie Boy 57, 61
Braddock, Rob 73
Brando, Marlon 27
Breaking Bad 6
Brooks, Albert 25
Bruckheimer, Jerry 147
Bunker, Edward 11
Burr, Jeff 11
Buscemi, Steve 85, 92
Byrne, Gabriel 25

Calderon, Paul 33-8
Camp, Joe 19
Campbell, Bruce 125, 127, 174
Cannon Films 20
Capra, Frank 137
Cashiers du Cinemart 179, 184, 185
Cayoutte, Laura 26
Chan, Jackie 81, 88
Chang, Terrence 103
Chaplin, Charles 134
Charlie's Angels 51
Chedwick, Jim 48
Chiba, Sonny 35, 93
Chick Flicks 21
Children of the Corn V: Fields of Terror 73
City on Fire 17, 136, 179-86
Clark, Greydon 179
Clockwork Orange 100
Clooney, George 126
Cochran, Steve 13
Coffy 51
Conrad, Joseph 49
The Conversation 122
Cop Land 33
Corbucci, Sergio 14
Corman, Roger 51, 176
Costner, Kevin 119
Creepshow 2 111
The Criminal Mind 57, 59
Crimson Peak 133
Crimson Tide 16, 119, 139, 146
Cronos 133
Curdled 73, 76

Dale, Dick 19
Dawn of the Dead 87, 111, 112
Dawson, Jeff 19

DC Comics 21
Dean, James 27
Death of a Gunfighter 14
Death Proof 39, 40-2
Debt Collector 20
De Niro, Robert 122, 139
De Palma, Brian 94
Del Toro, Guillermo 133-38
The Delfonics 6
Desperado 115
The Desperate Trail 103, 104, 109
Details 183
The Devil's Backbone 133
The Devil's Rejects 51, 173
Diamonds Are Forever 51
Dickens, Charles 6
Django Unchained 14, 111, 165
Django Unchained (comic) 45-9
Django/Zorro 165
Dreyfuss, Richard 25
Dukes of Hazzard 51
Duvall, Robert 138
Dylan, Bob 40, 49

E.R. 73, 76
Eastwood, Clint 125
Eddie Presley 173, 174
Edison, Thomas 4
Entertainment Weekly 21
Elmer Jones 45
Empire 180
Empire of the Steppes 49
Enemy of the State 122
Entertainment Weekly 103, 181
The Equalizer 33
Esposito, John 88
The Evil Dead 125, 132
Evil Dead 2 125

Index

The Faculty 128
The Fan 139
Fandango 58
Fat, Chow-Yun 103, 184
Feast 173
Ferlito, Vanessa 39
Film Threat 183
Film Threat Video Guide 182
Fine Arts Theater 26
Fisher, Terence 14
Flynn, Errol 95
Fonda, Bridget 95
Forrester, Robert 138
Four Rooms 33, 35, 37
Foxy Brown 51, 136
Freaky Deaky 64
Friday the 13th 111
From Dusk Till Dawn 87-90, 103, 111-7, 126, 132
From Dusk Till Dawn 2: Texas Blood Money 125-32, 173
From Dusk Till Dawn 3: The Hangman's Daughter 103-9
Frisell, Bill 49
Fulci, Lucio 88
Fuller, Samuel 137

Glamour 21
Godard, Jean-Luc 153
The Godfather 78
Gone with the Wind 36
Goodman, David 88
Google 10
Gore, Chris 182
Grier, Pam 52, 53, 138
Grindhouse 54, 111
Guera, R.M. 45-50
Gunsmoke 51

Hackman, Gene 149
Hadida, Samuel 141
Haig, Sid 51-6
Hamann, Craig 10, 57-62, 100, 101
Hammerhead 39
Hamsher, Jane 10, 97, 99, 101, 151
Harrell, Al 57, 62
Harrelson, Woody 98
The Hateful Eight 15, 17, 20, 168
Hawks, Howard 58
Hayek, Salma 116
Heathers 100
Hell Boy 133
Hell Ride 25, 28, 29, 30, 31
Hellman, Monte 63-6
Henricksen, Lance 130
Henschell, Todd 57
Hill, Jack 51
Hit List 130
Hitchcock, Alfred 94
Hitler, Adolf 43
Hopkins, Bo 127, 131
Hopper, Dennis 120
Hostel 42
House of 1,000 Corpses 51
Humbert, Dennis 67-72, 94
Hurt, William 78

I Dream of Jeannie 25
The Incredible Shrinking Critic 21
In the Line of Fire 130
Indiana Jones and the Temple of Doom 137
Inglourious Basterds 13, 15, 39, 41, 42-3, 46
Intruder 125
Ireland, John 13

Jackie Brown 5, 13, 17, 20, 51, 52, 53, 55, 64, 95, 128, 133, 138
Jackson, Michael 33
Jackson, Samuel L. 33, 34, 55, 120, 144, 173
Jaymes, Cathryn 10, 12, 13, 101
Joe the King 108
Jones, Angela 73-6
Joyner, C. Courtney 9
Judge Dredd 49

Kaplan, Jonathan 139
Karlson, Phil 9
Kasdan, Lawrence 78
Katzenberg, Jeffrey 148
Kaye, Linda 77-86, 95
Keaton, Michael 54
Keitel, Harvey 138, 140
Kill Bill 5, 15, 25, 28-30, 45, 51, 53, 122
The Killing 136
Killing Zoe 61, 111, 112
Killshot 119, 122
Kilmer, Val 120, 144
King Lear 153
King, Stephen 6
Kiss of Death 33
King of New York 33, 34
Kiss Me Deadly 22
KNB Efx 87, 111
Knightriders 111, 114
Kool and the Gang 19
Kubrick, Stanley 136, 137
Kung Fu 25
Kurtzman, Robert 87-90

LAByrinth Theater Company 33
Lam, Ringo 136, 179-86

Laverne & Shirley 25
Law & Order 33
Leary, Denis 25, 76
Lee, Danny 184
Leonard, Elmore 13, 64, 119, 122
Leone, Sergio 31
Lettich, Sheldon 10, 129
Lewis, Juliette 98
Lois Lane 21
Lolita 137
Lorre, Peter 37
The Lost Boys: The Lost Tribe 103
Lustig, William 130

The Mack 39
Macumba for Gringo 49
Mad Dog Time 25, 26
Madsen, Michael 28, 29
Mage 165
The Magnificent Seven 126
Malick, Terrence 121
Man on the Moon 73
The Man Who Shot Liberty Valance 68
Maniac Cop 130
Mantegna, Joe 25, 76
Martin, Dean 27
Martin, Strother 68
Martinez, Gerald 67, 69, 77, 79, 91
Martinez, Steve 77, 91-6
Marvel Comics 49
Marvin, Lee 68
McCarthy, Cormac 49
McGill, Scott 67, 151
McQueen, Steve 37
Menke, Sally 13
Miami Vice 33
Mimic 133

Index

Miramax 107
Mission: Impossible 51
Modesty Blaise 125
Monkey Trouble 138
Monsieur Verdoux 134
Morricone, Ennio 14
Mottini, Joao 48
MTV 182
Murder in the First 98
Murphy, Don 10, 16, 97-102, 151
My Best Friend's Birthday 16, 57-62, 77, 82, 97, 100, 151

Natural Born Killers 16, 58, 59, 77, 79-80, 88, 97-101, 114, 129, 132, 151
Navarro, Guillermo 133
Nero, Franco 14, 47
New Beverly Theater 14
The New York Daily News 21
New York Post 21
Nicholson, Jack 63
Nicotero, Greg 111, 116
Night of the Living Dead 87, 111

Oats, Warren 63
Ohmart, Ben 20
Oldman, Gary 120, 144
One Night with You 71
Oprah 21

Pacific Rim 133
Parks, Michael 105
Patrick, Robert 128, 131
Penn, Chris 107
Pesce, P.J. 103-10
Pesci, Joe 139
Pitt, Brad 42-3, 120, 145

Pitt, Ingrid 9
Playboy 46
Porky's 19
Polyi, Stevo 77
Pratt, Hugo 48
Premiere 23
Presley, Elvis 70, 94, 121, 158
Prison 9
Psycho 94
Psycho 2 94
Pulp Fiction 5, 15, 16, 17, 19, 20, 21, 23, 33-7, 51, 57, 61, 67, 73, 74-6, 77, 84, 89, 90, 108, 116, 133, 147, 169, 173, 179, 184

Q&A 34
Quentin Tarantino: The Cinema of Cool 19
Quentin Tarantino F.A.Q. 20
Quentin Tarantino: The Man and His Movies 19, 21
Quinn, Anthony 119
QTIII 20

Race with the Devil 87
Raimi, Sam 88, 125, 174
Real Steel 97
Rebel Without a Cause 27
Reiner, Rob 25
Relentless 130
Reservoir Dogs 5, 9, 10, 11-3, 15, 19, 23, 25-6, 34, 39, 59-60, 63-5, 73, 77, 84, 88, 90, 92, 107, 109, 111, 112, 122, 129, 133, 136, 140, 142, 156, 173, 177, 179
Return of the Swamp Thing 77
Revenge 119

Reynolds, Burt 95
Reynolds, Kevin 58
Rhames, Ving 35, 176
Richardson, Robert 30
Ride in the Whirlwind 63, 64
Rio Bravo 68
RKO Pictures 10
Road Racers 104
Rocco, Mark 98
Rocky 94
Rocky II 94
Rodriguez, Robert 55, 89, 103, 104, 105, 115, 133
Rolling Thunder Films 67, 69
Romero, George 111
The Rookie 125, 156
Roth, Eli 42
Roth, Tim 33
Rourke, Mickey 78, 79
Rum Punch 13
Russell, Kurt 41

Salem's Lot 19
The Savage Seven 25, 27, 28
Savini, Tom 111-18
Scalped 45, 46
Scorsese, Martin 7, 33, 138
Scott, Tony 16, 119-124, 140, 141, 148
Sea of Love 33
Self 21
The Session 25
Seventeen 21
The Seventh Sign 77
Shadow Warriors 93
She's Gotta Have It 152
Sherman, Dale 20
Shocker 77

Shoot 'Em Up 97
The Shooting 63
Siegel, Don 10, 14
Silverado 78
Sinatra, Frank 27, 29
Slater, Christian 95, 144
Smithee, Alan 14
Smokey and the Bandit 19
Smokin' Aces 2: Assassin's Ball 103
Sniper 3 103
The Sopranos 6
Spider Baby 51
Spiegel, Scott 9, 10, 14, 88, 125-32, 156, 173, 174
Spignesi, Stephen J. 5
Squeri, Rick 57
Stephen King's Graveyard Shift 88
Stewart, James 68
Stone, Oliver 98, 100, 101, 151
Stranger Than Paradise 152
Stripteaser 127, 174
Super Fuzz 19
Superman 19

Tales from the Hood 173, 176
Tenement 33
The Terror from Outer Space 136
Texas Riders 45
Then Came Bronson 105
Thiessen, Tiffani Amber 127
Thompson, Mike 180
Thou Shalt Not Kill, Except 129, 132
Thurman, Uma 5, 61, 91
THX 1138 51
Tierney, Lawrence 9, 10, 11-3, 173
The Today Show 21
Toi's 40, 61

Index

Top Gun 20, 123
Totten, Robert 114
Touchstone Theatre 33
Transformers 97
Travolta, John 35, 61, 86, 116, 138
True Romance 16, 22, 59, 63, 69-70, 88, 94, 119-23, 130, 139
Two Evil Eyes 111
Two-Lane Blacktop 63

Under the Shadowlight 49
Underworld 25, 26, 73, 76
Unforgiven 103
Unger, Bill 16, 139-50
Urban Comics 49
Used Cars 41

Video Archives 67, 70, 71, 77, 79, 91, 92, 94, 111
Vincent, Jan-Michael 130
Vossler, Rand 58, 77, 98, 151-64, 182
Vossler, Russell 77, 79, 151
Vox 183

Wagner, Matt 165-72
Walken, Christopher 120
Waltz, Christoph 47
Walsh, Raoul 10
Wafford, Roland 77
War Zone 57
Ward, Bumble 184
Warhol, Andy 6, 137

Washington, Denzel 149
The Waterboy 100
Wayne, John 14, 68
Weinstein, Bob 31, 125, 128, 177
Weir, Peter 183
Western Writers of America 14
Whaley, Frank 108
Where Eagles Dare 9
Whitaker, Duane 10, 127, 131, 173-8
White, Mike 17, 179-92
Who Do You Think You're Fooling? 17, 179, 182, 184
Wild Search 183
Wilson, Rob 46
Witness 183
Widmark, Richard 14
Wild in the Streets 25
The Wild One 27
Willis, Bruce 33, 35, 86
Wishmaster 87, 90
Woo, John 88, 103, 180
Woodard, Alfre 138

Yakin, Boaz 126, 173
You're Still Not Fooling Anybody 179

Zipper's Clown Palace 174
Zombie 87
Zombie, Rob 51, 55
Zorro 165
Zwang, Ron 10, 11

ABOUT THE CONTRIBUTORS

C. COURTNEY JOYNER is an accomplished screenwriter, director, and novelist.

STEPHEN J. SPIGNESI has written nearly sixty books on subjects as varied as Woody Allen to Stephen King. He is also an accomplished novelist.

JASON PANKOKE is the program director of the annual New Art Film Festival at the Art Theater Co-op in Champaign, IL, and editor of the regional film "local-'zine" *C-U Confidential*.

www.ingramcontent.com/pod-product-compliance
Lightning Source LLC
Chambersburg PA
CBHW061306110426
42742CB00012BA/2074